Getting Started with Dynamics 365 Portals

Best Practices and Solutions for Enterprises

Sanjaya Yapa

Apress®

Getting Started with Dynamics 365 Portals: Best Practices and Solutions for Enterprises

Sanjaya Yapa
Mount Waverley, VIC, Australia

ISBN-13 (pbk): 978-1-4842-5345-8   ISBN-13 (electronic): 978-1-4842-5346-5
https://doi.org/10.1007/978-1-4842-5346-5

Managing Director, Apress Media LLC: Welmoed Spahr
Acquisitions Editor: Smriti Srivastava
Development Editor: Laura Berendson
Coordinating Editor: Shrikant Vishwakarma

Cover designed by eStudioCalamar

Cover image designed by Pixabay

Distributed to the book trade worldwide by Springer Science+Business Media New York, 233 Spring Street, 6th Floor, New York, NY 10013. Phone 1-800-SPRINGER, fax (201) 348-4505, e-mail orders-ny@springer-sbm.com, or visit www.springeronline.com. Apress Media, LLC is a California LLC and the sole member (owner) is Springer Science + Business Media Finance Inc (SSBM Finance Inc). SSBM Finance Inc is a **Delaware** corporation.

For information on translations, please e-mail rights@apress.com, or visit www.apress.com/rights-permissions.

Apress titles may be purchased in bulk for academic, corporate, or promotional use. eBook versions and licenses are also available for most titles. For more information, reference our Print and eBook Bulk Sales web page at www.apress.com/bulk-sales.

Any source code or other supplementary material referenced by the author in this book is available to readers on GitHub via the book's product page, located at www.apress.com/978-1-4842-5345-8. For more detailed information, please visit www.apress.com/source-code.

Printed on acid-free paper

Table of Contents

About the Author

 **Sanjaya Yapa** currently works as a Microsoft Dynamics 365 CE/FS senior consultant in Melbourne, Australia. He has more than 12 years of experience in the industry, has been working with various Microsoft technologies since 2005, and possesses a wealth of experience in software design, development, team leadership, and product management. Sanjaya specializes in solution design and development with Microsoft Dynamics 365 CE/FS and application life cycle management with Azure DevOps. He is the author of *Customizing Dynamics 365* (Apress) and the co-author of *Effective Team Management with VSTS and TFS* (Apress).

You can contact him @sanjaya_yapa, and you can find his work at techjukebox.wordpress.com and almbox.wordpress.com.

About the Technical Reviewer

 **Scott Durow** is an experienced software architect and technologist with a passion for enabling business transformation through Microsoft technologies.

Scott is a Microsoft Business Applications MVP specializing in Dynamics 365. He is also the author of the Ribbon Workbench and SparkleXRM.

Find him on Twitter as @ScottDurow, and read his blog at scottdurow.develop1.net.

Acknowledgments

About six months ago, I took on the mammoth task of writing this book, and it would not have been possible without the kind support and help of many individuals. I would like to extend my heartfelt gratitude to all of them. A special thanks goes to Chaminda Chandrasekara, who has been an encouraging influence on me to move into this amazing world of authoring technical content. Also, I am thankful to Scott Durow for providing valuable technical reviews to make this book a success.

I would like to express my thanks and appreciation to my wife and daughter for encouraging me to achieve this milestone. I am also indebted to all my mentors for their guidance and encouragement and the opportunities given to me during my career.

Finally, I would like to express gratitude to my friends for their encouraging and inspiring words to move me forward.

Introduction

Ever since Microsoft bought ADX Studio and turned it into Dynamics 365, it has become the go-to portal technology for exposing Dynamics 365 CE functionality to external users. It has taken away the tedious task of deploying and maintaining web servers and applications simply because Dynamics 365 portals are part of the CE tenancy. As Dynamics 365 CE increased in popularity, the technical community started to publish blog posts about this new portal technology, and there are now an overwhelming number of articles available online.

The objective of this book is to provide a reference manual for the daily challenges faced by both intermediate and advanced Dynamics 365 CE consultants/developers. This book uses an example scenario throughout to explain the concepts and best practices. Therefore, it can also be considered as a hands-on guide to Dynamics 365 portals.

Specifically, Chapter 1 gives an overview of Dynamics 365 portals and provides insight into the history and evolution of Dynamics 365 portals. In this chapter, you will learn about the various types of portals available and get your first look at the example scenario presented throughout the book. Finally, the chapter introduces the portal features.

Chapter 2 takes you into the security aspects of Dynamics 365 portals. The chapter gives you a detailed guide to portal authentication and authorization techniques.

Chapter 3 starts with simple customizations such as making changes to the look and feel of a portal. The second part of the Chapter 3 is dedicated to explaining concepts such as entity forms and entity lists, which can be considered as the primary forms of implementing CRUD functionality in portals. Chapter 3 ends by explaining how to implement charts and validations.

Web forms and SharePoint integration are the primary focus of Chapter 4. Web forms are one of the least understood aspects of Dynamics 365 portals, so the chapter guides you with a real-world example. The second part of the chapter is reserved for explaining the SharePoint integration. The final section provides a quick overview to OData feeds and custom forms.

Chapter 5 and Chapter 6 are dedicated to liquid templates. Chapter 5 explains the basics of liquid templates, and Chapter 6 gives more examples of how to use liquid templates for advanced customization. It also gives you insight into the additional tools available for deploying and managing portal content.

This book provides a solid reference for your Dynamics 365 portal implementation needs. I hope this book is the first place you turn to solve any of your implementation challenges.

CHAPTER 1

Introduction

In general terms, a *portal* is an independent application that exposes selected data and functionality to external clients/users. Many businesses incorporate portals to get their clients more involved with the business, which reduces the cost of back-office administration, improves customer and supplier relationships, improves decision-making, and offers scalable licensing options. When businesses open up their processes to clients, there are so many parameters and constraints to be considered, which requires a staggering amount of designing and planning. Finally, when clients are getting more involved in such a way, companies have to spend less money on staffing because the client is empowered with the processes. For instance, almost every bank has an online client portal that enables clients to check their balances, pay bills, transfer money, apply for loans, and more.

This is not limited to the finance industry. Portals are heavily used in the energy, insurance, travel, and telecommunication industries, as well as in not-for-profit organizations. They use portals to improve their relationships with customers. These industries have a large customer base, and they can expose the self-service functionality to external users without any additional licensing costs. Also, not-for-profit organizations can easily set up fundraising campaigns and broadcast to larger audiences.

As more organizations are moving their applications to Dynamics 365, they are facing the hurdle of exposing some of the functionality to their external users. If an organization has a Dynamics 365 Enterprise

© Sanjaya Yapa 2019
S. Yapa, *Getting Started with Dynamics 365 Portals*,
https://doi.org/10.1007/978-1-4842-5346-5_1

subscription, then they possess at least one Dynamics 365 portal license. A Dynamics 365 portal can open a new gateway to end users to communicate and collaborate with the business by logging support issues, searching for knowledge about products and services, registering for events, booking holidays, viewing monthly bills and paying bills, and so on. A portal can be generated based on the target users, and even complex business processes can be implemented to meet specific business scenarios.

A significant advantage of using Dynamics 365 portals, when compared to other options such as WordPress, Power Platform, or custom Azure web sites, is that it is hosted, maintained, and integrated with Dynamics 365 CE. No additional hardware is required, no certificates are required, and there are no additional administration costs. Even for businesses that already have a web site, a Dynamics 365 portal will extend the capabilities of the existing web presence. Dynamics 365 portals come with out-of-the-box templates and can be extended and further customized. We will be discussing these templates in this book.

Important   As per the licensing guidelines effective October 2018, access to the first included portal for the tenant requires the purchase of ten Enterprise user licenses (Dynamics 365 CE Plan or Dynamics 365 Applications). For more information, please refer to the licensing guidelines at `https://mbs.microsoft.com/Files/public/365/Dynamics365LicensingGuide.pdf`.

Community Portal for Customer Engagement

A community portal template is an ideal platform for your superstar customers to give you good feedback about your products and services and for attracting potential clients. Also, these portals can be used to identify the potential client requirements of a product or service and make improvements. You might also want to share future product/service developments with your clients to get their feedback, and a community portal will help you in such scenarios. For instance, you could publish a blog article about the product enhancements coming in the next few months to capture what your customers think about them and further enhance the product. The users can comment on these blog posts with their feedback and expectations.

Internal Staff Engagement

An employee portal is well suited when you have occasional Dynamics 365 users. For example, say a group of employees will be using Dynamics 365 every now and then for some limited functionality. An employee portal could be configured to expose this limited functionality to this particular set of employees. The functionality can even be extended for the employees to raise tickets for support. Keep in mind that, as per the licensing guidelines, any internal users indirectly accessing the Dynamics 365 data via a portal are required to have an appropriate Dynamics 365 license.

Partner Engagement

Configuring a partner portal will enable you to capture sales channel data from your business partners like with your internal sales staff. For instance, use a partner portal to empower your most trusted partners to generate new opportunities and allow them to manage the opportunities they create. These partners can even be external sales agents who help you promote your business and keep that additional sales pipeline flowing with more opportunities and leads.

Custom Portals

There will always be complex scenarios where the existing portal templates may not fit in, and in such situations, the custom portal framework can be used to implement that additional complexity. This framework is completely extensible and customizable, and it gives you an instant starting point by minimizing the initial development and setup costs. For instance, in an event management scenario, you could require additional customizations when it comes to registrations and advertising, so a custom portal is the most suitable in such situations. For facilitating these complex and unique scenarios, you could use the existing page templates and combine them into a custom portal.

Note   As you can see, the primary difference between each of these portals is in how they present the data. Each portal is intended for different purposes, and they are capable of presenting data to the target external audience and interacting with them according to the intended purpose of the portal.

How It Began

In early stages of Dynamics CRM, there was a limited online presence compared to today. In most cases, the systems were handled by the internal staff. But with the development of the Internet over the years, these requirements have changed. A simple customer relationship management (CRM) tool will not be enough to stay ahead of the competition. New ways of client interactions have come to the market, and everyone is keen on acquiring these new toys. For CRM implementations, the necessity of a portal is now more important. In early implementations of Dynamics CRM, most of the time the clients had to develop a web front end and interact with the CRM system. In some scenarios, content management systems (CMSs) such as Orchard were used to fulfil this need.

One such CMS that was specialized to develop portals for Dynamics CRM was the Canadian-based ADX Studio, which was built on top of ASP. NET and SQL Server. ADX Studio, partnering with Microsoft initially, released a free version, which is known as Portal Accelerators. In 2015, Microsoft announced it had fully acquired the product, and it became Dynamics 365 portals. The biggest benefit of this acquisition was the portal was built right into Dynamics 365 without any dependency on third-party CMS technology. The CMS was built into Dynamics 365 as a unified interface application (Figure 1-1). This application is extremely user-friendly, and even a power user can simply create content without any extensive knowledge about the app.

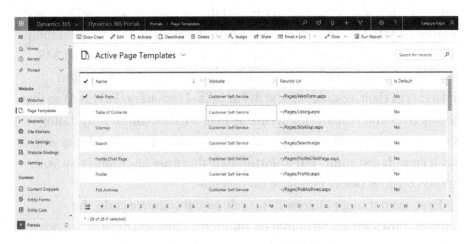

Figure 1-1. *Dynamics 365 portals unified application*

There are other portal options for Dynamics 365 portals. The next section will have a quick overview of the options available.

Other Portal Options

We can probably all agree that the current trend is to move to the cloud, and Microsoft encourages end users to do so. But at this moment, there are a ton of Dynamics 365 on-premise customers. They have many barriers to overcome before moving to the online world, no matter how good it is, and this situation is not going to change anytime soon. Since the Dynamics 365 portals functionality is an offering to online customers, it is not going to solve the portal requirements of on-premise customers. So, what are the options available to on-premise customers?

Portal Source Code Releases

Microsoft released the source code for Dynamics 365 portals version 8.3 under an open source license to support the customers who are in legacy versions of ADX Studio to migrate easily to the cloud and to support their on-premise clients. Adoxio, the company that created ADX Studio CMS, created a GitHub project known as xRM Portals Community Edition (https://github.com/Adoxio/xRM-Portals-Community-Edition) so that the bug fixes and enhancements are available to the community. Using this, you can create your own portal and customize and extend it as you like. It sounds awesome, but unfortunately there are few things that you should consider before choosing this avenue.

First, even though Microsoft has released the source code, the solutions provided are all managed solutions; plus, you have to provide your own web servers. Within these managed solutions, there are plug-ins and custom workflow activities that we do not have the source code for that might not work with your Dynamics 365 on-premise deployment. In such scenarios, there is no easy way to modify the code. The other issue is that even though Microsoft has released the code, it does not provide any support. There is some support provided by Adoxio and its partners, but you will have to rely heavily on the community.

This approach is really good for upgrading from ADX Studio v7, where the customers have made substantial investments into custom code. Moving to the xRM Portals Community Edition is a much better option if you have any plans to migrate to the online version of Dynamics 365 CE and portals. But this is not recommended for new projects, because at some point in the future, this avenue will be closed.

Third-Party Portals

The purpose of this section is not to give any endorsements about the products listed here, but to provide a reference of third-party portal tools. For instance, there could be scenarios where a current on-premise system has a customer portal developed using one of the solutions listed. In such situations, understanding the current implementation is crucial in future online migration scenarios.

- **SiteCore**: This ISV provides a connector known as Microsoft Dynamics 365 Sales Connect that allows you to map your data to the SiteCore portal. This is designed to manage the customer information in Dynamics 365 CE and synchronize the data and behavior of the portal.

- **AlexaCRM**: This is a framework created in PHP and a WordPress plug-in that allows you to interact with Dynamics 365 CE. As we all know, WordPress is a popular platform that is used for blogging, for content sharing, and even as a CMS.

- **The Portal Connector**: This is an add-on to Sitefinity, which is an ASP.NET content management system. The Portal Connector add-on allows you to present Dynamics 365 data on a web site and allows you to create and edit records.

- **Webcurl**: This is based on Drupal and has a Webcurl CRM Connector for Dynamics 365 CE. This will synchronize the Dynamics 365 CE and the portal.

No matter how good these options are, the recommendation for Dynamics 365 CE Online is to go with the Dynamics 365 portal functionality unless you are in on-premises and do not have any plans to migrate to the Dynamics 365 CE Online version because of internal barriers in the near future. The biggest hurdles when adopting Dynamics 365 portals are the resources and the knowledge required. But the community is getting more knowledgeable about Dynamics 365 portal functionality, so it is worth investing in.

Custom Portals

There is always the option for you to develop a portal from scratch. All of the ISVs mentioned earlier do not have distinct access to Dynamics 365 CE. Every connector of these platforms uses the standard CRM SDK to interact with Dynamics 365 CE. One of the best options is to use ASP. NET MVC with the CRM SDK. But, keep in mind at the time of writing this book, the Dynamics 365 SDK does not support .NET Core. This option is worth considering if you have web development experience and if none of the third-party solutions fits your requirements. Then again, if you implemented your system on Dynamics 365 CE Online, then why spend the time and money on custom development? You already have one Dynamics 365 portal ready to be configured.

Benefits of Using a Dynamics 365 Portal

It is always good to understand the benefits of portals before moving any further. As mentioned earlier, there is no hardware cost because the portal is integrated with Dynamics 365 CE and every Enterprise subscription will have at least one portal license. The following are some of the other benefits that you could practically achieve with portals:

- You can present data to your clients in real time with minimal effort. As soon as you submit the changes, they will be available to your clients.

- Security can be easily configured, since it is within the same platform and allows access to the information based on the access levels assigned to the clients.

- External identity providers enable authenticated users to connect with multiple external IDs.

- Content management is easy; it is the same as creating and updating regular Dynamics 365 CE records.

- You can easily represent a Dynamics 365 form in a portal with a few clicks; even a power user can configure a data entry form that can be used to enter data.

- Document storage in portals is seamless. You can easily configure the forms to use the notes, and they will be available to portals straightaway. Extending this further by enabling Azure Storage allows you to provide high-capacity file storage. Dynamics 365 CE integration with SharePoint can be exposed with portals and allows users to view, upload, delete, and download documents from the portal.

The benefits are seemingly endless.

9

The Example Scenario

In this book, when introducing the features of Dynamics 365 portals, I will give detailed examples. These examples are based on the following scenario.

In this scenario, the Small Businesses Membership Association wants to extend the functionality of its Dynamics 365 CE implementation to its users. One such application is the event management segment of the association. In the marketing app, there is an event management portal available that you can configure, but to demonstrate the examples, this book will use a custom event management portal. For further information, refer to https://docs.microsoft.com/en-au/dynamics365/customer-engagement/marketing/event-management.

The Small Businesses Membership Association organizes events throughout the year and targets different audiences based on a client's business industry. For instance, the association organizes events for agriculture businesses and would like the members with such businesses to benefit from the event. The internal event management staff will organize the events using the Dynamics 365 CE application. When an event is set up and finalized, the event details will be visible to the client. Clients register via the portal.

The following are the features available via the portal to the client:

- When the event management staff organizes and approves the event, the event should be accessible to the members.

- On the member portal, it should list the events relevant to the member's business industry.

- There will be general events that all the members can attend, and the association expects such events to be displayed to all the members.

- When the event reaches the registration end date, then online registration will be disabled.

- The available events should be listed as a tile with an image to get the member's attention.

- The registration should be disabled when it reaches the maximum number of seats available for the event.

- The registrant should be able to see the event program when selecting the event.

- A registrant should be able to pay online or pay at the gate for the event.

- A client should be directed to the payment gateway for online payments.

- If the event is for more than one day, the registrants should be able to book accommodations. When booking accommodations, clients must first register for the event and then book the accommodations to get the special pricing.

- There are events where the registrant should be able to bring one or two guests, and the price will be calculated and displayed to the registrant based on the number of guests they are bringing.

- In such scenarios, the registrant must provide the details of the guests.

- Once the registrations are completed, the registrant can download the tickets from the site.

- A registrant should be able to cancel the registrations.

- A registrant should be able to add guests to and remove guests from the registration. Once the payment is completed and the registration is completed, registrants cannot alter the registration.

- A client should be able to enter their dietary preferences, which will enable the caterers to prepare the menu.

- When an event is at the planning stage, the organizers will open the draft to the various partners to provide quotes for the venue, accommodations, food, and so on.

- Event venue providers and caterers should also be able to use this partner portal to provide details about their facilities and get approval for a given event.

- Partners have a different portal, where they can submit their quotations, and once the quotations are approved, the partners will be notified via the portal.

Figure 1-2 illustrates the high-level entity relationship diagram for this example application. As per this example, to have more functionality, we are going to use a custom portal where we can do further customizations as per the requirements mentioned earlier.

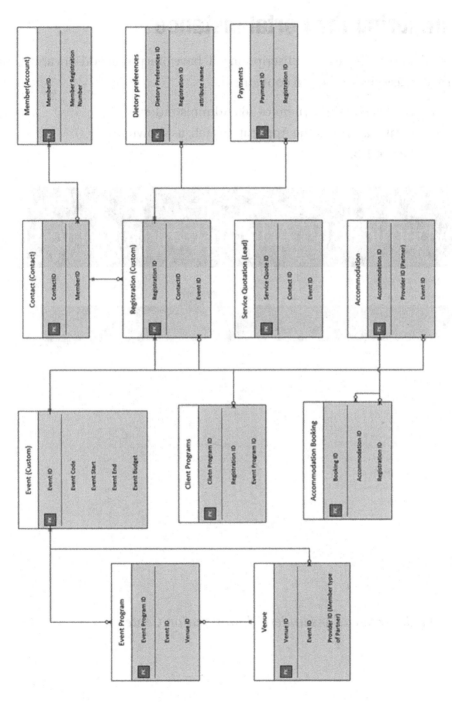

Figure 1-2. *Entity relationship diagram*

Configuring the Portal Instance

As mentioned earlier, every subscription will have one portal add-on, and with a few easy clicks, you can configure it.

1. Navigate to the Dynamics 365 Administration Center and click the Applications tab, as shown in Figure 1-3.

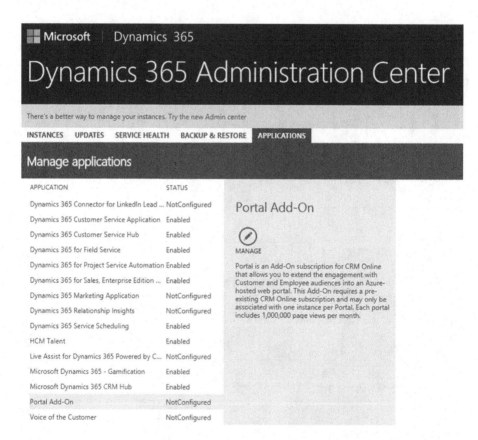

Figure 1-3. *Applications under Administration Center*

As you can see in Figure 1-3, the Portal Add-On status is NotConfigured. To configure the portal, click the Manage icon on the top of the Add-On description pane on the left. This will take you to the Portal Configuration Wizard, as shown in Figure 1-4.

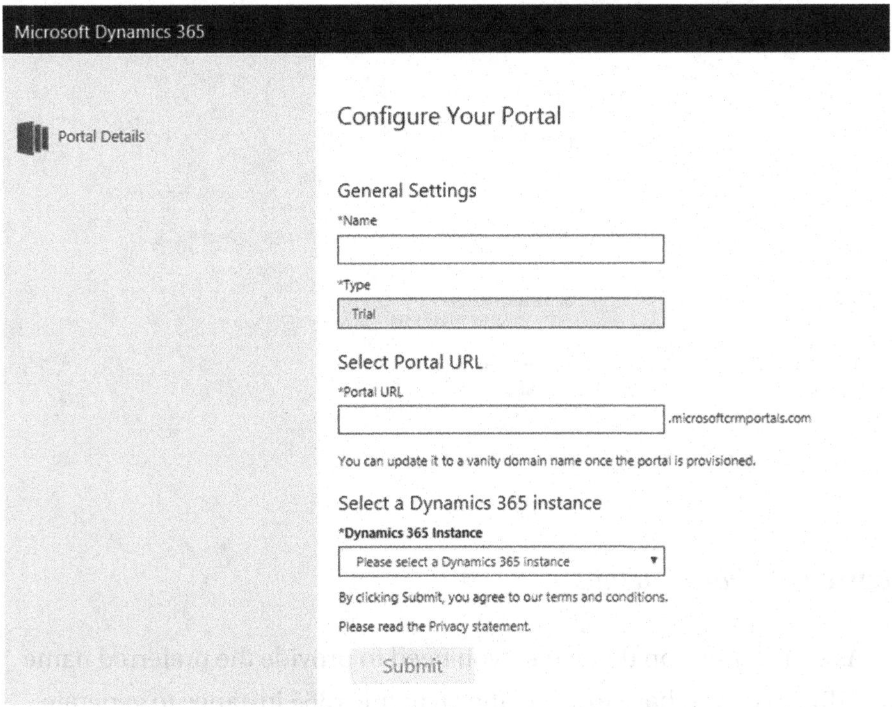

Figure 1-4. *Portal Configuration Wizard, start screen*

Enter the details of the portal, as shown in Figure 1-5. For demonstration purposes, we will be using a Dynamics 365 CE 30-day trial.

15

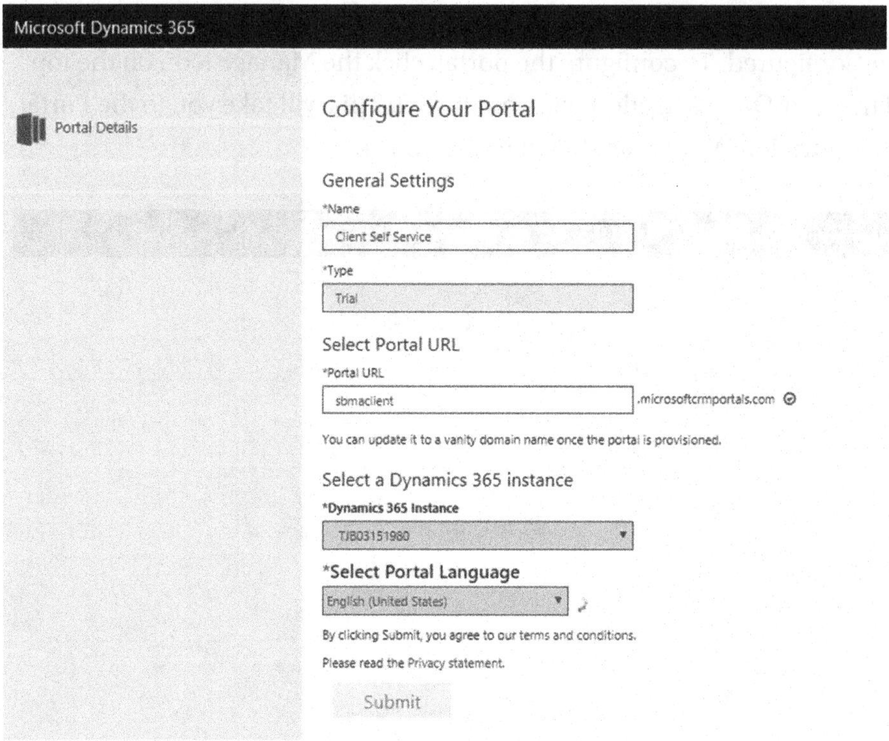

Microsoft Dynamics 365

| Portal Details | Configure Your Portal |

General Settings

*Name

Client Self Service

*Type

Trial

Select Portal URL

*Portal URL

sbmaclient   .microsoftcrmportals.com ⊘

You can update it to a vanity domain name once the portal is provisioned.

Select a Dynamics 365 instance

*Dynamics 365 Instance

TJB03151980   ▼

*Select Portal Language

English (United States)   ▼ ↗

By clicking Submit, you agree to our terms and conditions.

Please read the Privacy statement.

Submit

Figure 1-5. *Portal details*

As you can see, on this screen you need to provide the preferred name and URL. Also, you have to select the Dynamics 365 instance to generate the portal. After entering the details, click the Submit button, and it will load some additional settings that you need to provide before moving forward. For instance, you need to provide the following (Figure 1-6):

- The portal administrator

- The target audience

- The portal type

- Whether the portal will get an early upgrade

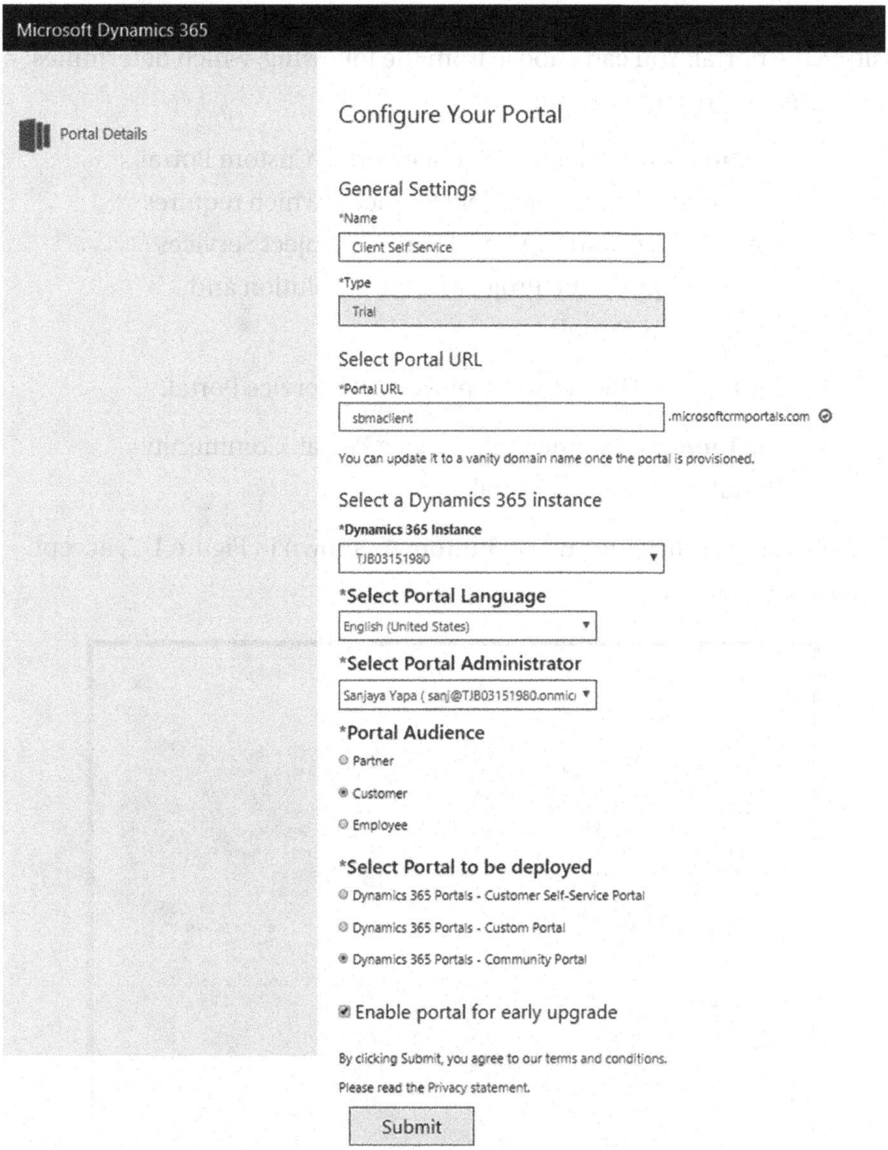

Microsoft Dynamics 365

Portal Details

Configure Your Portal

General Settings

*Name

Client Self Service

*Type

Trial

Select Portal URL

*Portal URL

sbmaclient   .microsoftcrmportals.com

You can update it to a vanity domain name once the portal is provisioned.

Select a Dynamics 365 instance

*Dynamics 365 Instance

TJB03151980

*Select Portal Language

English (United States)

*Select Portal Administrator

Sanjaya Yapa (sanj@TJB03151980.onmic

*Portal Audience

○ Partner

● Customer

○ Employee

*Select Portal to be deployed

○ Dynamics 365 Portals - Customer Self-Service Portal

○ Dynamics 365 Portals - Custom Portal

● Dynamics 365 Portals - Community Portal

☑ Enable portal for early upgrade

By clicking Submit, you agree to our terms and conditions.

Please read the Privacy statement.

Submit

Figure 1-6. *Portal configuration information*

The Portal Audience section defines the type of audience who will be visiting the portal. You can choose from the following, which determines what options you will be given:

- **Partner**: Customer Self-Service Portal, Custom Portal, Partner Portal, Partner Field Services (which requires Field Service Solution), and Partner Project Services (which requires the Project Services Solution and Community Portal).

- **Employee**: This is the Employee Self-Service Portal.

- **Customer**: Customer Self-Service Portal, Community Portal, and Custom Portal.

Now you can click the Submit button. As shown in Figure 1-7, accept the terms of service.

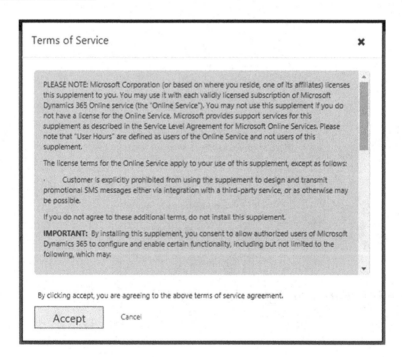

Figure 1-7. *Terms of Service page*

Generally, it might take few minutes to complete the configuration. You will see the message in Figure 1-8 on the screen.

Microsoft Dynamics 365
Portal Details
Diagnose and resolve problems
Your request has been submitted and request id is d1866ff7-44fe-4352-9164-2e425251df52. This request might take some time to finish, so please click here after some time to see the status.

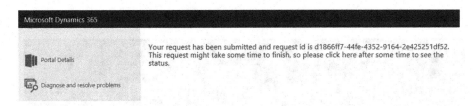

Figure 1-8. *Configuration in progress*

As instructed in the message, click the link (on the word *here*) to refresh the page. You will be taken back to the details page, and a message will be displayed to indicate that the portal is currently being configured (see Figure 1-9).

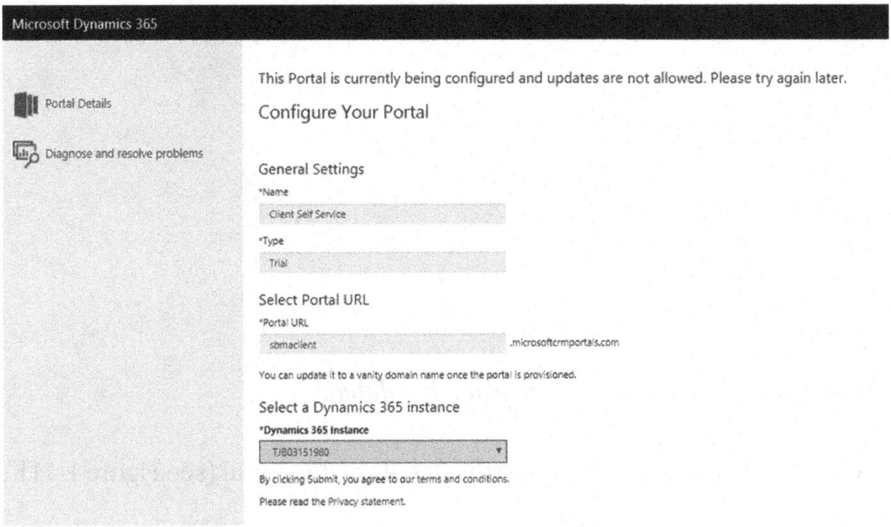

Microsoft Dynamics 365
Portal Details
Diagnose and resolve problems
This Portal is currently being configured and updates are not allowed. Please try again later.
Configure Your Portal
General Settings
*Name
Client Self Service
*Type
Trial
Select Portal URL
*Portal URL
sbmaclient
.microsoftcrmportals.com
You can update it to a vanity domain name once the portal is provisioned.
Select a Dynamics 365 instance
*Dynamics 365 Instance
TJB03151980
By clicking Submit, you agree to our terms and conditions.
Please read the Privacy statement.

Figure 1-9. *Portal configuration in progress message*

Give it some time, and once the portal is configured, you will see the status change to Configured when you navigate to the Dynamics 365 Administration Center (see Figure 1-10).

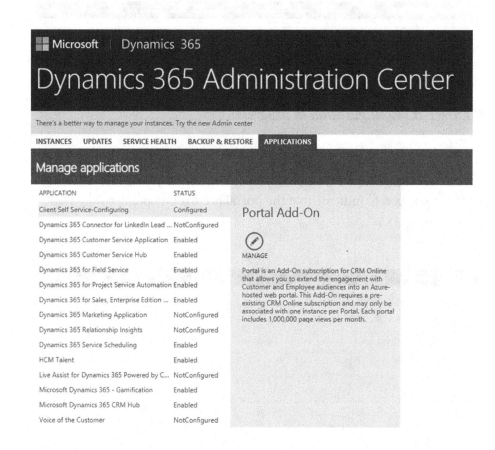

Figure 1-10. *Portal configuration completed*

Click the Manage button to see the details of the portal (see Figure 1-11).

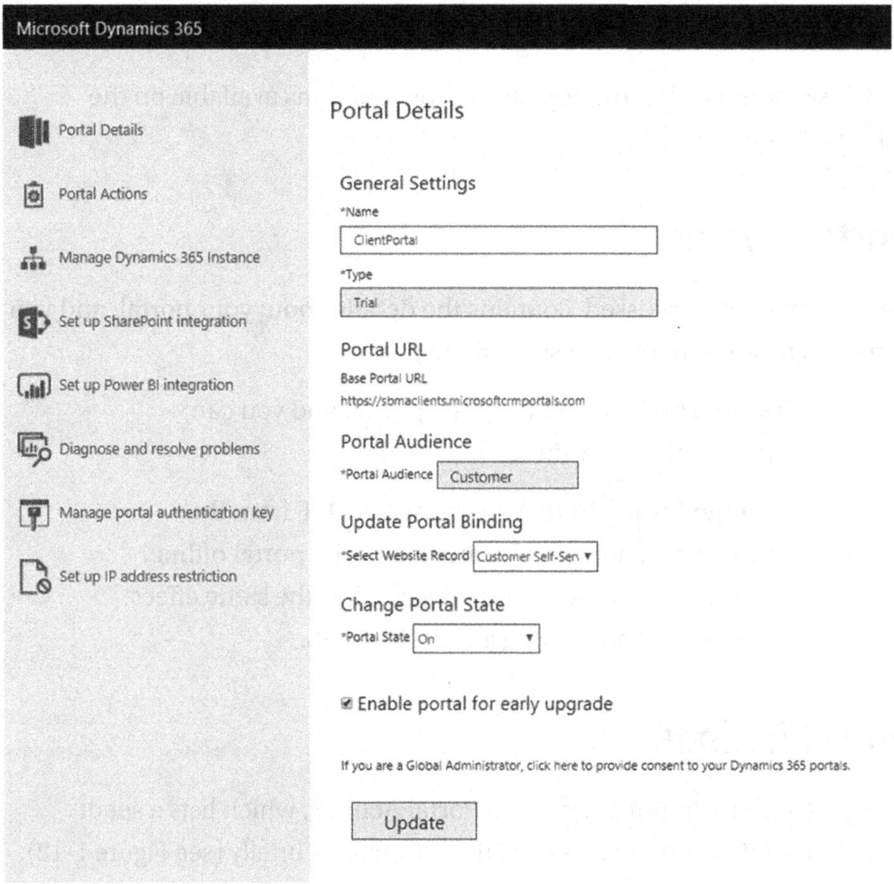

Figure 1-11. *Portal Details page after configuration*

As you can see, there are some functions available to you. Based on the requirements, you can configure these additional services and features.

Dynamics 365 Portal Features

In this section, I will introduce each of the functions available on the Administration Center page.

Portal Details

The first page, as discussed, contains the details about your portal, and you can change portal name and state of the portal.

- **Name**: This is the name of the portal, and you can update this at any time.

- **Change Portal State**: You can select OFF from the drop-down and click Update to take the portal offline. Turning the portal off and on again has the same effect as stopping and starting a web site in IIS.

Portal Actions

The next administration function is Portal Actions, which lists a set of admin-related actions. Let's look at these functions briefly (see Figure 1-12).

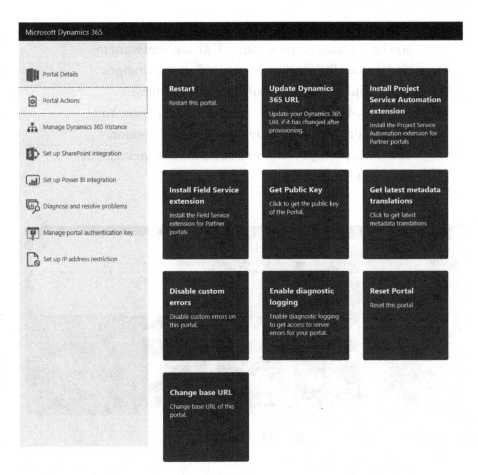

Figure 1-12. *Portal Actions page*

- **Restart**: This is similar to restarting a web page hosted in IIS. When you click this, a confirmation message will pop up to inform you that the web site will be unavailable for a few minutes. If this is OK, then click Restart. This allows you to hard clear the cache.

- **Update Dynamics 365 URL**: Assume a scenario where you have changed the instance URL and you want to update the URL for the portal to reflect the changes. This happens when the company name changes because of acquisitions or rebranding scenarios. You simply click the Update Dynamics 365 URL option, and it will prompt you with a confirmation message, as shown in Figure 1-13.

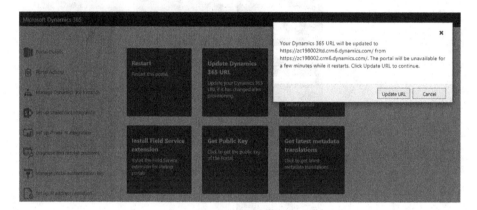

Figure 1-13. *Confirming the URL change*

- Click Update URL, and it will take few minutes for the changes to take effect. Once that is done, you must restart the portal with the option explained earlier.

- **Install Project Service Automation extension**: This is useful in scenarios where you are using the Project Services add-on and you want external stakeholders to interact with the ongoing project work. The following URL provides more details about the features available with this feature: `https://docs.microsoft.com/en-us/dynamics365/customer-engagement/portals/integrate-project-service-automation`. Please note that your portal must be a Partner portal to enable this feature.

- **Install Field Service extension**: If you are using Field Services, then you can install this extension to collaborate and expose field service-related information to partners. For this feature to work, your portal must be a Partner portal. You can find more details about the feature at `https://docs.microsoft.com/en-us/dynamics365/customer-engagement/portals/integrate-field-service`.

- **Get Public Key**: Downloading the public key will enable you to connect with Live Assist by CafeX to provide a chat solution to authenticated users. For further information, please visit `https://docs.microsoft.com/en-us/dynamics365/customer-engagement/portals/get-public-key`.

- **Get latest metadata translations**: During the installation of portal, the portal-related solutions are installed, and the solution metadata translations (for instance, field name, form name, view name, and so on) are installed only for the languages activated in the Dynamics 365 organization. In a situation where you are activating a new language, the metadata will not be installed automatically. To get the metadata translations, you must import them from the Dynamics 365 Administration Center page.

- **Disable custom errors**: As we all know, web developers will extensively debug their applications to ensure the implementations are correct. To troubleshoot issues, you can access the detailed error logs of the portal. For instance, during development or troubleshooting, it is beneficial to see the details of the error that is commonly known as the *yellow screen of death* (YSOD). When you use this option and disable the custom errors, you will see the YSOD when an error occurs. Once the error is fixed, you can reenable it. This is kind of a toggle button, which will turn into "Enable custom errors" after the automatic refresh. To enable custom errors, click this button.

- **Enable diagnostic logging**: This feature enables you to log errors after you publish the portal for your clients. To access the portal logs, you can configure the portal to send all the error logs to Azure Blob Storage, which makes it easier to troubleshoot client-reported errors. When you click this option, you will be asked to provide the blob storage connection string, and by default, the retention period is set to 30 days. See Figure 1-14.

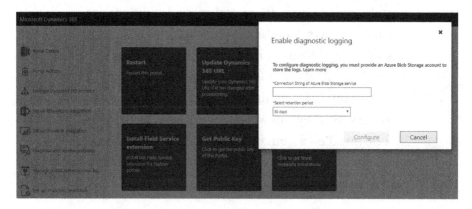

Figure 1-14. *Enabling diagnostic logging*

A telemetry-logs blob container is created once the configuration process is completed. We will look at this feature in detail later in this book.

- **Reset Portal**: There could be scenarios where you want to delete resources in your provisioned portal. You can achieve this by resetting the portal, which will delete all the hosted resources associated with it. Then you can provision the portal again. Keep in mind that when you reset the portal, the portal configuration or any solutions associated with Dynamics 365 CE will remain as it is. Here you need to keep in mind that the portal configuration data is kept separate from the business-related data. Once the reset is complete, then the URL will no longer be available. This option is available when the portal is partially configured and fails due to some internal errors. Please visit the following URL for additional information: `https://docs.microsoft.com/en-us/dynamics365/customer-engagement/portals/reset-portal`.

- **Change the base URL**: You can change the base URL of your portal after it is provisioned. For instance, if your portal URL is `https://sbmaclients.microsoftcrmportals.com` at the time of provisioning the portal, you might want to change it to `https://clients-sbma.microsoftcrmportals.com` based on the customer requirements. So, you could use the previous URL for another portal that you have provisioned. Sometimes this might fail and is considered a transient error. You can retry it, and if the issues continue, it is advisable to contact Microsoft Support.

Managing a Dynamics 365 Instance

After provisioning the portal, you have the option to change the instance
(see Figure 1-15).

Figure 1-15. *Changing a Dynamics 365 instance*

Once you click the Update Dynamics 365 instance, you will be
presented with the screen shown in Figure 1-16 to set the details of the new
instance.

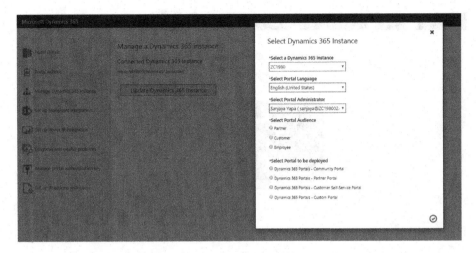

Figure 1-16. *Selecting a Dynamics 365 instance*

The nice thing about these settings is that they are self-explanatory.

Setting Up SharePoint Integration

As we all know, the number-one choice for document management is
SharePoint, and you can integrate the portal with your online SharePoint
account. Once the "Set up SharePoint integration" feature is enabled, the
portal will be enabled for uploading and displaying documents to and
from SharePoint directly. I cover this feature in detail later in this book. See
Figure 1-17.

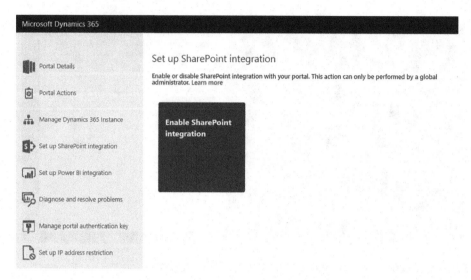

Figure 1-17. *Enabling SharePoint integration*

Enabling Power BI Visualization

Power BI provides advanced reporting and dashboards with interactions to the end users. To provide this awesome feature to your end users, you must enable it. More information will be provided later in this book. See Figure 1-18.

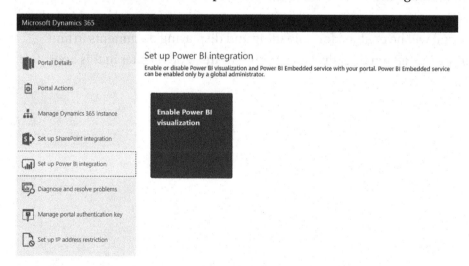

Figure 1-18. *Enabling Power BI visualizations*

Diagnosing and Resolving Problems

A self-service diagnostic tool known as the Portal Checker enables the portal administrators to identify common issues in the portal and proactively troubleshoot them. Use the "Diagnose and resolve problems" option and then click the "Run diagnostics" button in the middle of the screen (see Figure 1-19).

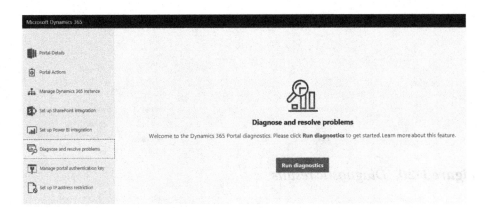

Figure 1-19. *Running the diagnostics tool*

You will see a plethora of information about the portal's health. You can expand an issue to dive deep into the diagnostic steps, as shown in Figure 1-20.

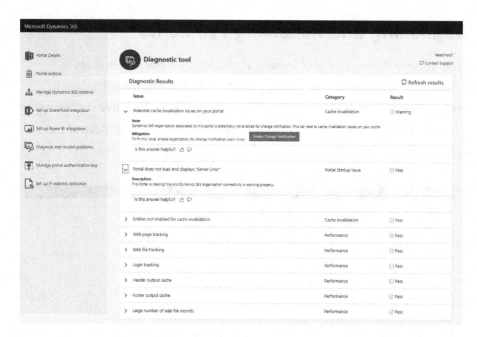

Figure 1-20. *Diagnostic results*

Managing the Portal Authentication Key

The portal you provision will be connected to Dynamics 365 through an Azure Active Directory application. This is created in the same tenant where the portal is provisioned and registered during the provisioning of the portal. Each portal that you provision has a separate Azure Active Directory application. An authentication key is generated during the provisioning process, and the public part of the key is automatically uploaded to the Azure Active Directory application. Keep in mind that this key will expire in every two years, so you must update it; otherwise, the portal will stop working. You can update the key using the "Manage portal authentication key" option. See Figure 1-21.

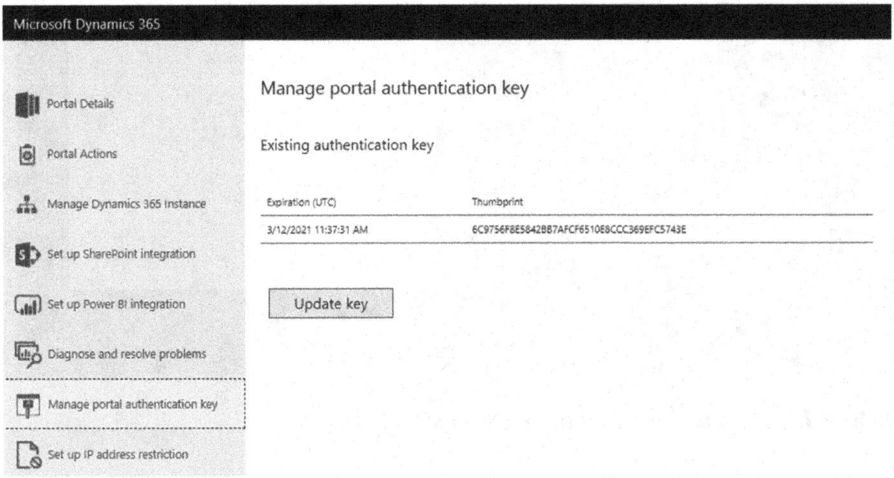

Figure 1-21. *Portal authentication key*

Setting Up IP Address Restrictions

When the portal is provisioned, it is accessible by everyone from any computer. Sometimes you might be asked to restrict this unlimited access to the portal. You can easily do this by using the "Set up IP address restriction" feature. When you add IP addresses to this list, then the portal will be accessed only through those IP addresses. When a request comes in, it is evaluated with this list, and if the IP where the request originated is not listed, then an HTTP 403 error will be displayed to the requester. See Figure 1-22.

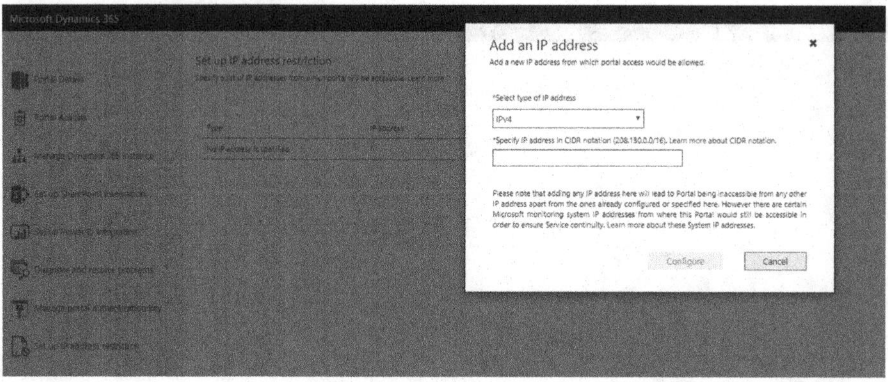

Figure 1-22. *Applying IP address restrictions*

Summary

In this chapter, I discussed four main topics. First, I discussed how Dynamics 365 portals began and some details about Dynamics 365 portals and options. Second, we looked at the example scenario that will be used in this book, and next we set up an example portal. Finally, once the portal was set up, we discussed the admin functions available for managing the portal. In the next chapter, we will be looking at the content management application and configuring portal security.

CHAPTER 2

Portal Security and Content Management

The purpose of this chapter is to guide you through the portal security and content management interface of Dynamics 365 portals. There are several approaches that you can take to configure portal security. Portal security does not work the same way as Dynamics 365 security works. The challenge is to grant the right access to resources, content, and data whether you have done an advanced configuration or a simple configuration. Therefore, careful planning must be done beforehand. In this chapter, you will learn how to configure security and when to use these configurations. Figure 2-1 is a high-level illustration of how portal security works.

© Sanjaya Yapa 2019
S. Yapa, *Getting Started with Dynamics 365 Portals*,
https://doi.org/10.1007/978-1-4842-5346-5_2

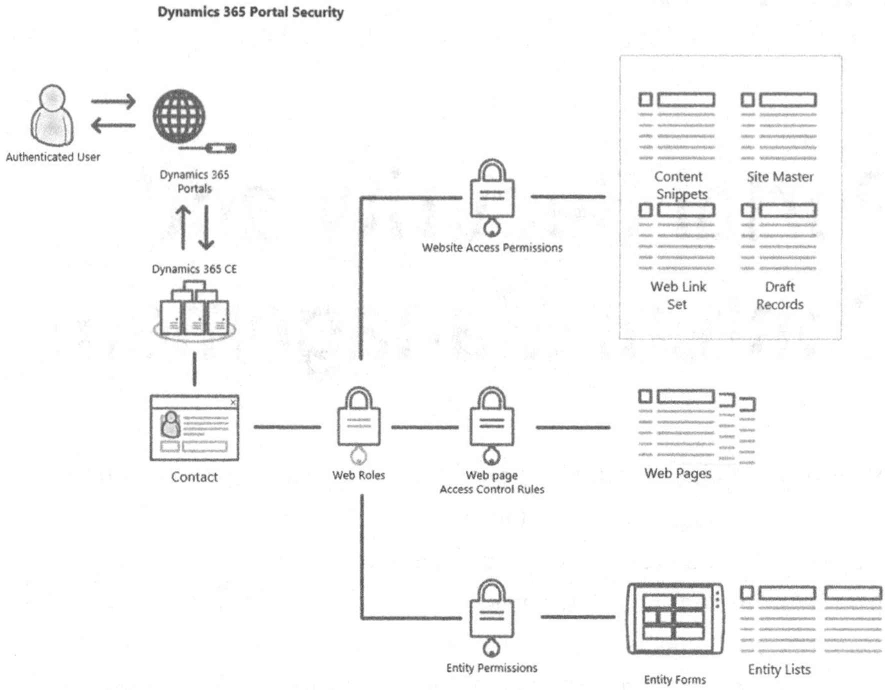

Dynamics 365 Portal Security

Figure 2-1. *Overview of Dynamics 365 portal security*

Portal Security Concerns

As mentioned, when thinking about security, we have to think about these three things: data, content, and web resources. Also, based on the customer requirements, there are several types of users coming into your portal. They can be anonymous users; customers, partners, or suppliers; power users or senior admin staff; and administrators or technicians. During the planning stage, you must determine the level of access that should be granted to these different categories of users. Consider the following when determining this:

- Anonymous users should be given the least amount of access, meaning only the public content.

- The customers, suppliers, or partners should be able to log in to the portal and submit and modify their own data.

- Power users or senior admin staff might want more sensitive information in the decision-making process or when serving the clients. As an example, granting membership to a club might require additional approval based on the data provided in the application.

- The most secure level is handled only by the administrators or any other authenticated users or internal staff.

The hierarchy should flow from the least security to most security. That is, the pages should be stacked top to bottom with the least secure pages at the top and the most secured pages at the bottom. As of now, the authentication can be configured in two ways: with local authentication and with external authentication.

- Local authentication uses the contact records of Dynamics 365 for Customer Engagement for authorization. This is implemented through the common form-based authentication.

- The ASP.NET Identity API is used for implementing external authentication, which includes user credential management done through a third-party identity provider. This includes Google, Yahoo, and OAuth 2.0–based providers such as Microsoft, Facebook, and Twitter. When configured, the external identity will have the same access as the internal identity.

You can use invitations and trigger confirmation e-mails with both these approaches. Portal administrators have the ability to enable or disable any of these combinations through the Site Settings. As explained, when you configure a portal, by default the contact-based authentication is configured. In the next section, let's look at the capabilities of the contact-based authentication approach.

Contact-Based Authentication

This is considered to be the simplest form of authentication you will get with Dynamics 365 portals; it uses the contacts of the Dynamics 365 for Customer Engagement organization.

Register a User

Let's assume a scenario where a contact of the Small Businesses Membership Association (SBMA) wants to register via the portal and is planning to participate in one of the events organized by the association. When you navigate to the portal and click "Sign in," you will be taken to the login page, which has three tabs: Sign-in, Register, and Redeem invitation. Figure 2-2 shows the Register tab.

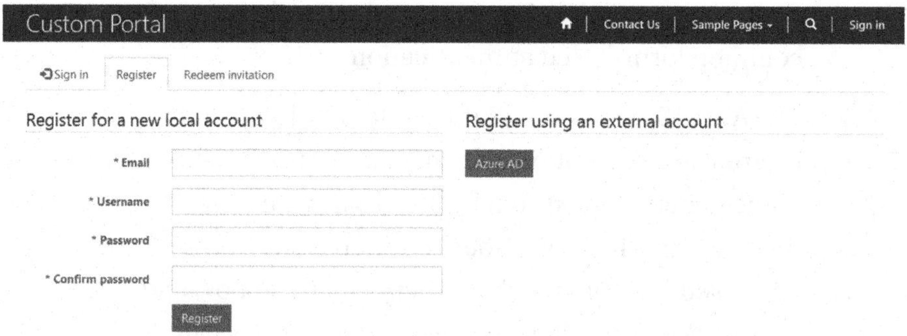

Figure 2-2. Login page of the portal

Let's enter some data to register and see what happens. The user will be taken to the Profile page, as shown in Figure 2-3, where they can enter their personal details. On this page, users can update the details and change their e-mail and password. Also, the "Manage external authentication" option lists the configured external authentication provider that the user account is associated with.

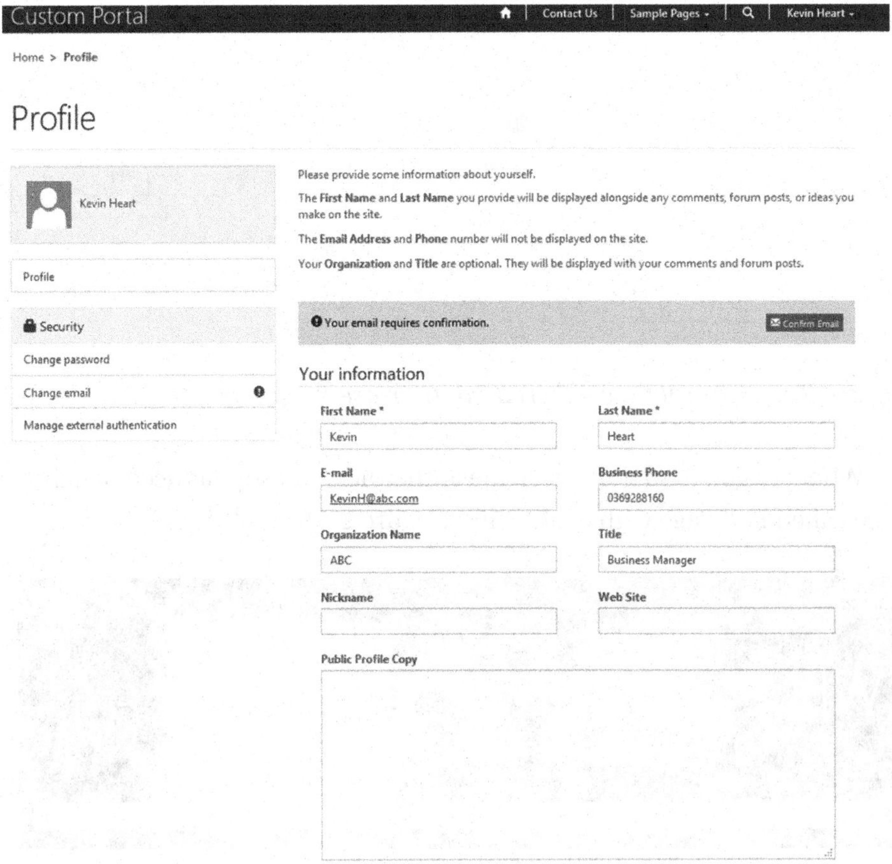

Figure 2-3. *Contact's Profile page*

When the user registers, the user will be created as a contact, as shown in Figure 2-4, and this user can navigate around the portal with limited access to the data and resources.

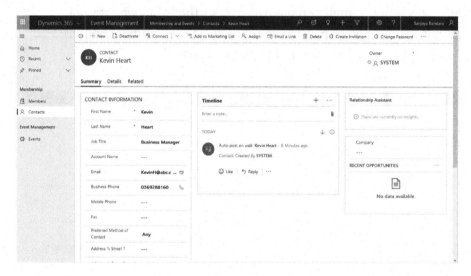

Figure 2-4. *Contact record created after user registration*

When logged in to the portal, the authenticated user has access to the page called Full Page with Child Links (Figure 2-5).

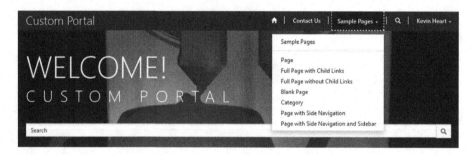

Figure 2-5. *Pages accessible to the authenticated user*

The authenticated user can click the link and navigate to the page (Figure 2-6).

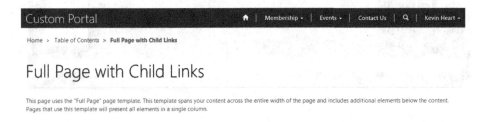

Figure 2-6. *Authenticated user accessing web page*

But this page is hidden from anonymous visitors. When an anonymous user tries to access the web page, they will be redirected to the login page asking for credentials (Figure 2-7). This is enforced using web page access controls, which we will discuss later in this chapter (in the section "Control Web Page Access for Portals").

Figure 2-7. *An anonymous users cannot see this page*

When a user with administrative access logs in, they can access anything and even use the web content editor (Figure 2-8).

Figure 2-8. *System admin login*

Now there is a new editor available for system administrators (Figure 2-9). Please note that at the time of writing this book, this editor is in preview mode. You can learn more about the new content editor at https://docs.microsoft. com/en-us/dynamics365/customer-engagement/portals/portal-new-content-editor.

Note   Microsoft has most recently introduced PowerApps Portal, which enables organizations to create low-code portal solutions for their external customers and allows them to interact with Common Data Sources. Microsoft has also started merging the capabilities offered by the Dynamics 365 for Customer Engagement portal with PowerApps Portal. For further reading, please visit https:// powerapps.microsoft.com/en-us/blog/introducing-powerapps-portals-powerful-low-code-websites-for-external-users/.

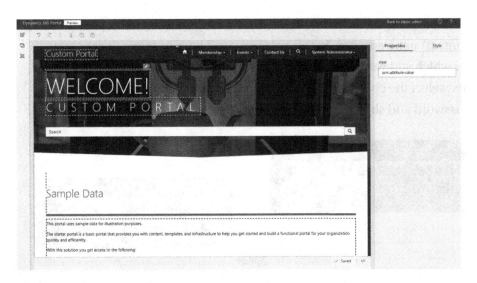

Figure 2-9. *New portal editor*

We will be discussing the content editor later in this book. An internal staff member who has access to the contacts can easily change the password of the contact. On the command ribbon of the Dynamics 365 interface, click the "Change password of the portal contact" option (Figure 2-10).

Figure 2-10. *Changing the password for a contact*

On the right side of the screen, the "Change password for portal contact" pane appears. In this pane, you will have to select the contact for which you want to change the password. As illustrated in Figure 2-11, first select the contact from the lookup and click Next. Finally, change the password and share with the contact via a separate e-mail.

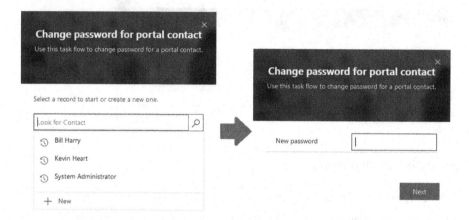

Figure 2-11. *Selecting a contact from the lookup and changing the password*

Please note that the password is visible, and it is always a good practice to advise the contact to change it at the next login. In the next section, you will look at external authentication.

External Authentication

As mentioned at the beginning of this chapter, portal visitors and contacts can also be authenticated via third-party authentication providers. The following are the supported external authentication providers:

- Microsoft
- Google

- Yahoo

- Facebook

- Twitter

- LinkedIn

Note   For the brevity of this book, I will be discussing the configuration of the Microsoft and Google authentication providers. For other provider configuration, please visit `https://docs.microsoft.com/en-us/dynamics365/customer-engagement/portals/configure-oauth2-settings`. Also, note that you can specify multiple providers so that the visitors can select the one they most prefer.

The external identity providers that are based on OAuth 2.0 require you to register an application to acquire the client ID and client secret. Most of the time, when registering the application, the redirect URL to the portal must be specified so that the user will be redirected back to the portal. Then, in the portal's Site Settings, this client ID and the client secret are configured to establish a secure connection between Dynamoics 365 portals an the external identity provider. First, let's look at how to set up Google as the external identity provider.

Google

1. Navigate to Google Developer Console: `https://console.developers.google.com`. You will be requested to log in using your Google credentials. You can select an existing project, or you can create a new project, as shown in Figure 2-12.

Figure 2-12. *Creating a new Google API project*

2. Click New Project to create a new project. You can
    enter a new project name or leave the default one
    and click Create (Figure 2-13).

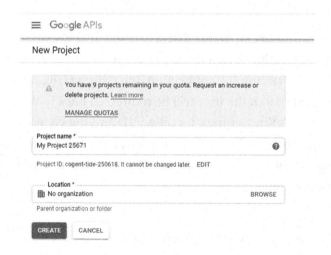

Figure 2-13. *Creating a new project*

3. Navigate to the Credentials section and click Create
    Credentials, as shown in Figure 2-14. From the
    drop-down options, select OAuth Client ID.

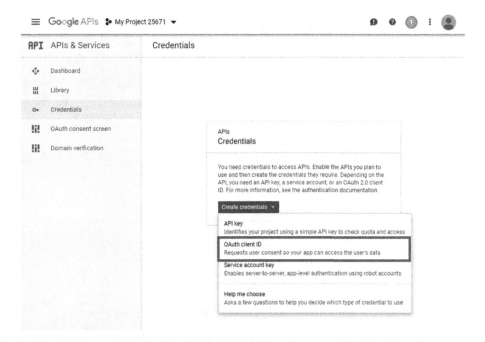

Figure 2-14. *Creating credentials*

4. Then you will be directed to the form to select the
    application type. From the options, select Web
    Application. This will display the form shown in
    Figure 2-15. You also need to enter the following
    entries:

    a. **Authorized JavaScript origins**: This is the URL of the portal/
       web page where your request originates.

    b. **Authorized redirect URIs**: This is the callback URL that will
       be used to redirect the user once the request validation is
       successful.

    After entering these values, click Create.

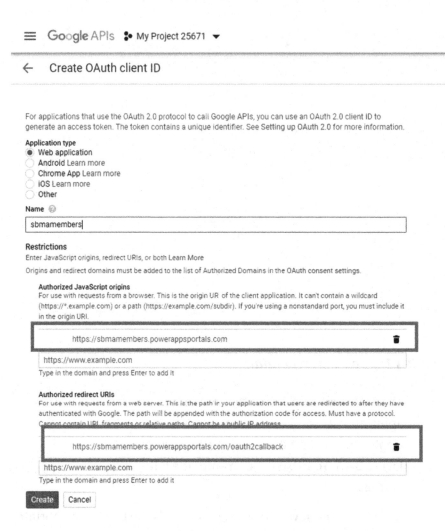

Figure 2-15. *Selecting an application type*

5. Now the credentials are created, and you will
    be prompted with the client ID and client secret
    (Figure 2-16).

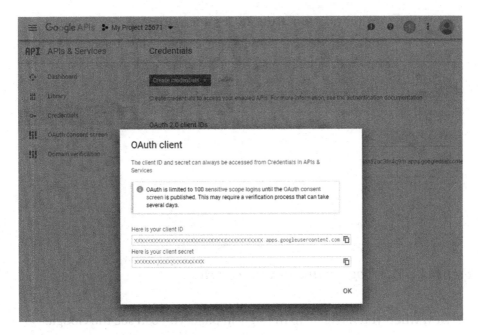

Figure 2-16. *Client ID and client secret*

You need to take note of the client ID. The client secret
is not required here.

6. Once all this is done, you must update the Site
Settings of the portal. Navigate to Portals and
then to Site Settings. The following are the entries
you should set up. These settings have the format
of Authentication/OpenIdConnect /<provider>
/<Setting>. The provider will be used as the caption
on the login screen.

- **Authentication/OpenIdConnect/Google/Authority**:
  This is the URI to get the authentication token.

- **Authentication/OpenIdConnect/Google/ClientId**:
  This is the client ID generated when you created the
  credentials, which is registered with the Google API.

49

- **Authentication/OpenIdConnect/Google/
  RedirectUri**: This should be the same value that
  you enter when registering the Google API.

Figure 2-17 illustrates the values entered in Site Settings.

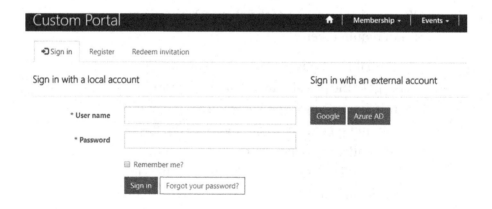

Figure 2-17. *Google authentication entries*

Now when you navigate to the sign-in page, you can see the Google
"Sign-in" button, as illustrated in Figure 2-18.

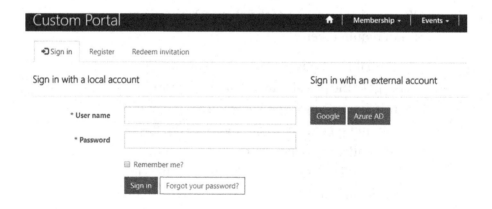

Figure 2-18. *Google "Sign-in" button*

When the end user clicks the Google button, the user will be directed
to the Sign in with Google prompt (Figure 2-19).

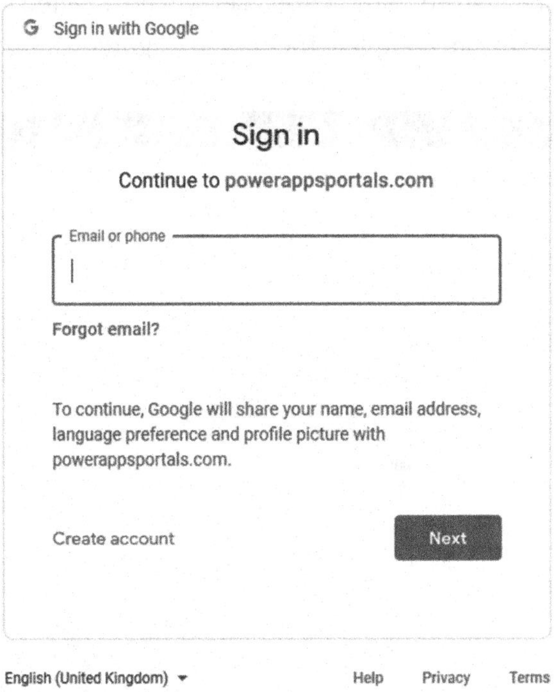

Figure 2-19. *Sign in with Google prompt*

After entering an e-mail and clicking the Next button, the user will be directed to the portal page to enter the e-mail address to register, as shown in Figure 2-20.

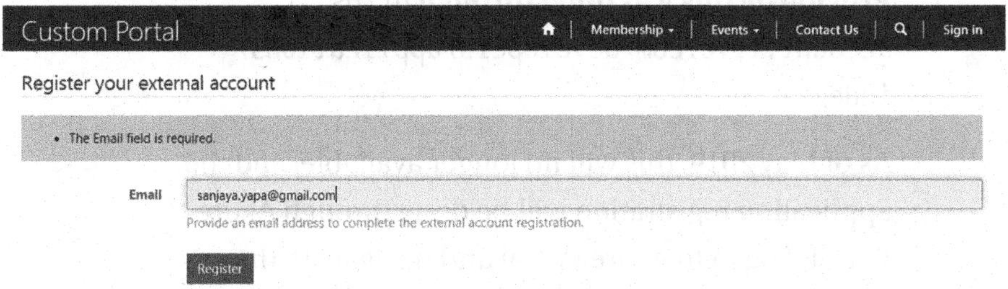

Figure 2-20. *Registering with a Google e-mail address*

When click the Register button, the user will be directed to the Profile page, where the user can complete the profile (Figure-2-21).

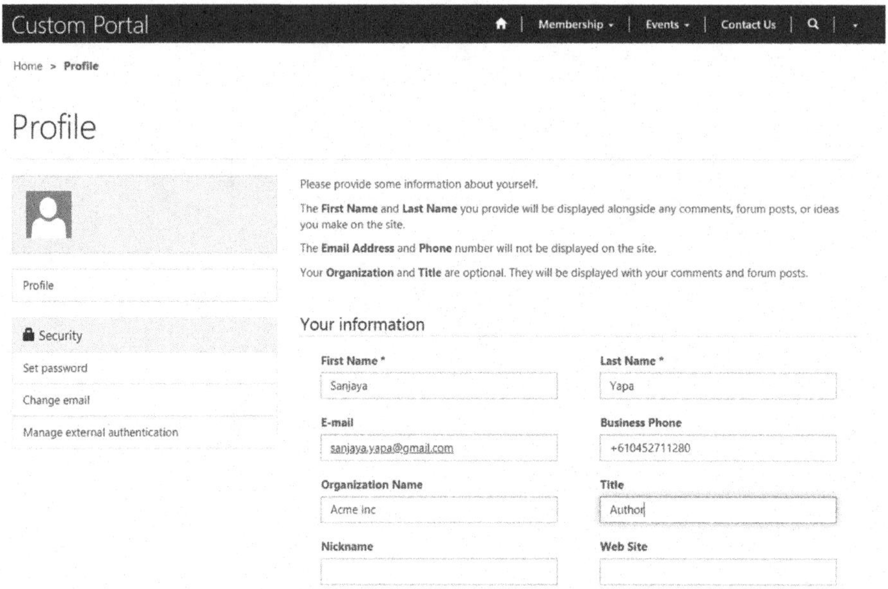

Figure 2-21. *Profile page*

You can see the "E-mail address" field is populated with your Gmail address.

Microsoft

1. **Previously this was done through** https://
   account.live.com/developers/applications/
   index.

   As of May 2019, this will no longer available, and the application registration will be done through Azure Portal. Log in to Azure Portal and navigate to the App Registration section. Navigate to the "Owned applications" tab, as shown in Figure 2-22.

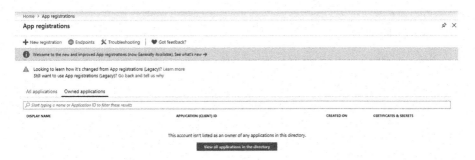

Figure 2-22. *Creating the app registration*

Note   App registration was replaced in May 2019.

---

2. Click the +New registration and enter the following
    fields:

    a. Name of the application.

    b. "Supported account types" determines what type of accounts
        have access, and for this example, we will be selecting the
        third option: "Accounts in any organizational directory and
        personal Microsoft accounts (e.g., Outlook, Skype, Xbox)."

    c. Finally, specify the redirect URL. The redirect URL is
        important for most authentication scenarios. As discussed,
        this URL will be used to return the authentication response.

    After filling the form, click Register (Figure 2-23).

53

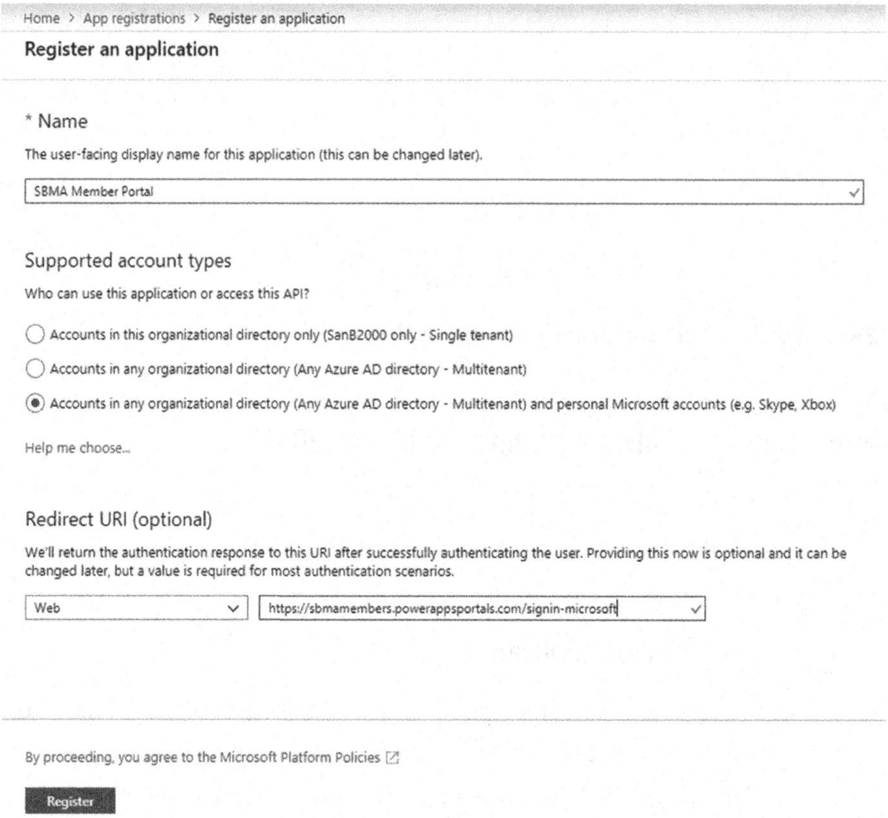

Home > App registrations > Register an application

Register an application

---

* Name

The user-facing display name for this application (this can be changed later).

SBMA Member Portal

Supported account types

Who can use this application or access this API?

○ Accounts in this organizational directory only (SanB2000 only - Single tenant)

○ Accounts in any organizational directory (Any Azure AD directory - Multitenant)

◉ Accounts in any organizational directory (Any Azure AD directory - Multitenant) and personal Microsoft accounts (e.g. Skype, Xbox)

Help me choose...

Redirect URI (optional)

We'll return the authentication response to this URI after successfully authenticating the user. Providing this now is optional and it can be changed later, but a value is required for most authentication scenarios.

| Web | https://sbmamembers.powerappsportals.com/signin-microsoft |

By proceeding, you agree to the Microsoft Platform Policies ☑

Register

Figure 2-23. *Registering the application*

Once the application is successfully registered, you will
be redirected to the screen shown in Figure 2-24.

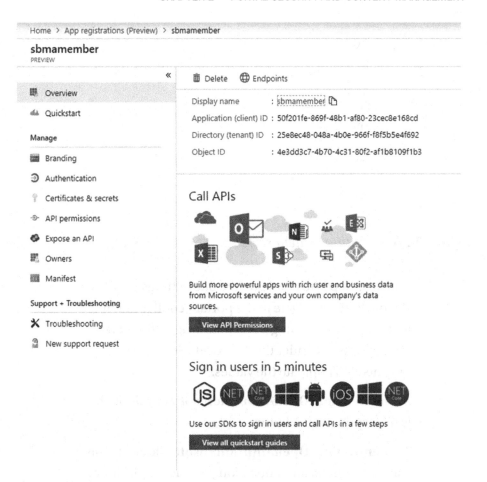

Figure 2-24. *Registered application overview*

On this form, you can see that the application ID is displayed. When you register the application, you will not get a client secret. The client secret must be generated, and it can be done by going into "Certificate & secrets."

3. Under "Certificate & secrets," click "Create a new secret," as shown in Figure 2-25. Specify the name and the expire settings.

Figure 2-25. *Creating a client secret*

4. The next step is to configure the Site Settings
    (Figure 2-26). Navigate to the portal's configuration
    and then to Site Settings. The following settings are
    already entered under the Active Site Settings; you
    only need to populate the values.

    Authentication/OpenAuth/Microsoft/Caption: This
    is the caption of the button.

    Authentication/OpenAuth/Microsoft/ClientId: This
    value is from the authentication provider application.
    You can find the client ID on the Overview page.

    Authentication/OpenAuth/Microsoft/ClientSecret:
    This value is from the authentication provider
    application. You need to enter the client secret you've
    generated here.

Figure 2-26. *Microsoft authentication settings*

5. Navigate to the sign-in page of the portal; you will see the Microsoft button as an external sign-in option (Figure 2-27).

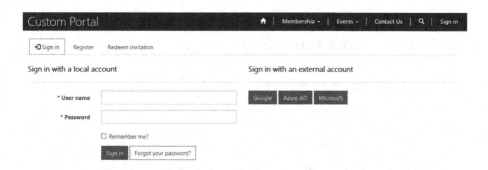

Figure 2-27. *Sign-in page with Microsoft authentication*

6. Click the Microsoft button, and it will prompt you to enter your Microsoft ID (Figure 2-28). As usual, enter the e-mail and password.

Figure 2-28. *Microsoft login screen*

On the next screen (Figure 2-29), you must let the application access your information; click Yes to continue.

Figure 2-29. *Allowing the application to access your information*

As shown in Figure 2-30, you will be asked to register your external account by entering your e-mail.

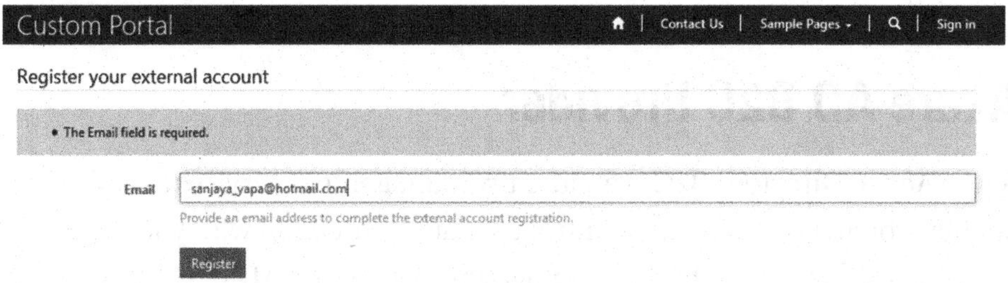

Figure 2-30. *Registering your e-mail*

Click the Register button, and you will be directed to the profile page, as shown in Figure 2-31.

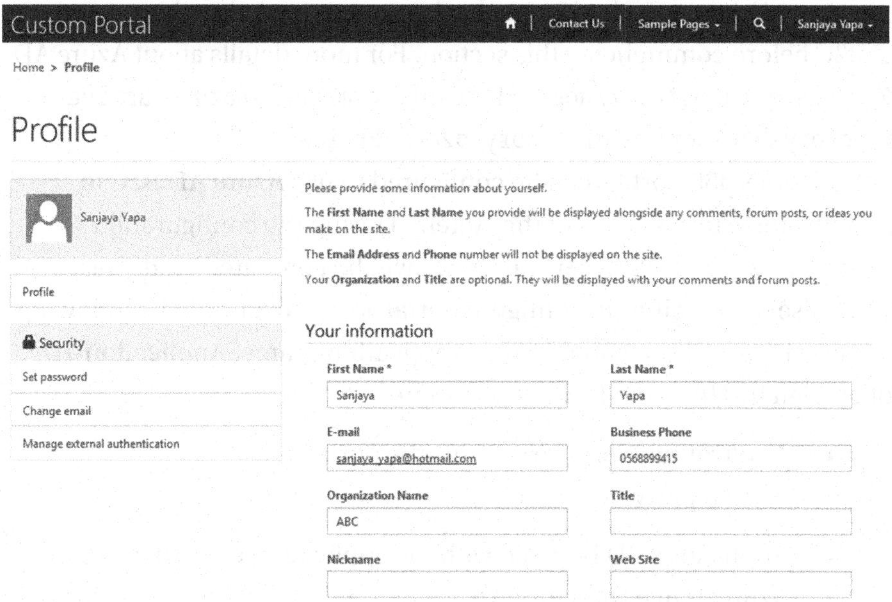

Figure 2-31. *Profile page for the externally authenticated user*

Similar to this, you can configure the other external authentication providers based on your client requirements. In the next section, you will look at the Azure AD B2C configuration.

Azure AD B2C Provider

Azure Active Directory B2C is an identity management service that enables you to configure and control user authentication with your web, mobile, desktop, or single-page application. The Azure AD B2C allows the users of your application to sign up, sign in, edit profiles, and reset passwords. This authentication mechanism is built on the OpenID and OAuth 2.0 protocols, which use a security token to provide secure access to your application. This book will look at how Azure AD B2C can be used to provide authentication to your Dynamics 365 portals. It is highly recommended that you have some background knowledge about Azure AD B2C before commencing this section. For more details about Azure AD B2C, please visit `https://docs.microsoft.com/en-us/azure/active-directory-b2c/active-directory-b2c-overview`.

Dynamics 365 portals can be configured to use Azure AD B2C to authenticate external users of the system. During the configuration process of Azure AD B2C, several values will be generated, and you should use these values to configure portal authentication. The following are the values that you should note: Application-Name, Application-ID, Policy-Sign in-URL, and Federation-Name.

- Application-Name represents the portal as a trusted party.

- Application-ID is linked with the application created in Azure Active Directory B2C.

- Policy-Sign in-URL is the issuer URL specified in metadata endpoint.

- Federation-Name is the distinctive name to identify the B2C provider and is used with Site Settings to group configuration settings for this specific provider.

Create an Azure AD B2C Tenant

As the first step, you must create an Azure AD B2C tenant. First sign into the Azure Portal (Figure 2-32).

1. Next, choose "+Create a resource" in the top-left corner of the portal and search and select Active Directory B2C.

Figure 2-32. *Azure Active Directory B2C home page*

2. Click the Create button. On this screen, enter the relevant details and click Create at the bottom-right corner of the screen (Figure 2-33).

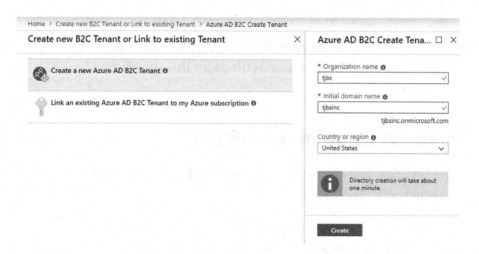

Figure 2-33. *Creating an Azure AD B2C tenant*

3. As the next step, click the "Link an existing Azure
    B2C Tenant to my Azure Subscription" and enter the
    details, as shown in Figure 2-34.

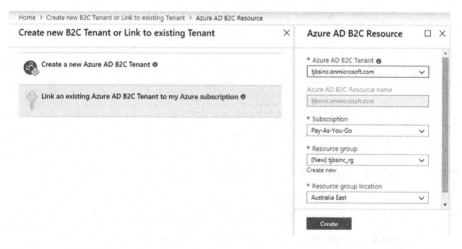

Figure 2-34. *Linking an existing Azure AD B2C tenant to you Azure
subscription*

4. Before starting to use the tenant, you must make sure that you are using the directory that contains the tenant. Click the subscription page, and the Global Subscription filter will be shown on the right side of the browser window. Switch the directory if required (Figure 2-35).

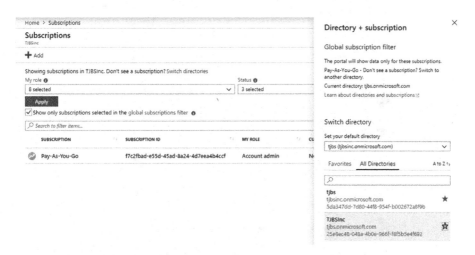

Figure 2-35. *Switching the directory*

5. The next step is to register the application. On the Applications tab, click +Add, as shown in Figure 2-36.

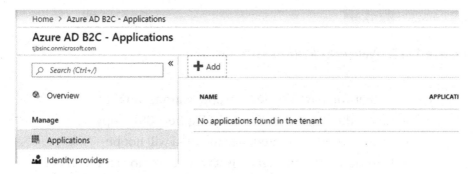

Figure 2-36. *Adding a new application*

On the next screen, enter the name of the application and select Yes for both "Include web app/ web API" and "Allow implicit flow." Also, set the reply URLs as shown in Figure 2-37.

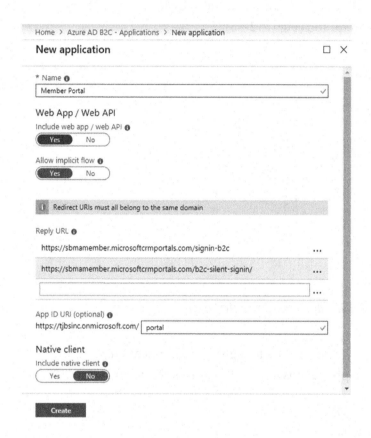

Figure 2-37. *New application settings*

6. Now that you have created the application, you must generate the key on the Keys tab (Figure 2-38). Copy the value when generated, because you will not be able to view the value again. But you can remove the existing one and can always generate a new one.

Figure 2-38. *Generating a key*

7. The next step is to create the sign-up and sign-in
    policy. This is done through user flows. You can
    learn more about user flows from the following
    link: https://docs.microsoft.com/en-us/azure/
    active-directory-b2c/active-directory-b2c-
    reference-policies#create-a-sign-up-or-
    sign-in-policy. Select User Flows from the left
    pane and click +Create New in the toolbar. On the
    next screen (Figure 2-39), you will see three tabs:
    Recommended, Preview, and All. You should start
    by selecting the user flow type. For this example, we
    will be selecting recommended flows, which can be
    used for most applications.

Home > Azure AD B2C - User flows (policies) > Create a user flow

Create a user flow   ✕

Select a user flow type

A user flow is a series of pages for your users to interact with to sign up or sign into their account. Choose one to start with and you can create multiple user flows to define your entire authentication experience for your app. Learn more about user flow types.

Recommended   Preview   All

Recommended for most applications.

Sign up and sign in	Profile editing	Password reset
Lets a user register for or log into their account	Lets the user configure their user attributes	Allows a user to choose a new password after verifying their email

Figure 2-39. *Selecting a user flow type*

8. On the Create screen, there are a few mandatory
    fields that you should fill in. First, you should enter
    the name, which is a unique string to identify the
    user flow requests to Azure AD B2C (Figure 2-40).

Note   Since this is a lengthy form, each section will be explained
separately.

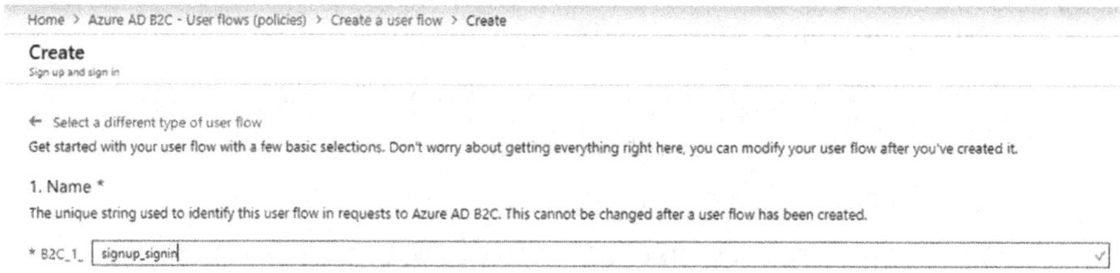

Home > Azure AD B2C - User flows (policies) > Create a user flow > **Create**

Create
Sign up and sign in

← Select a different type of user flow
Get started with your user flow with a few basic selections. Don't worry about getting everything right here, you can modify your user flow after you've created it.

1. Name *
The unique string used to identify this user flow in requests to Azure AD B2C. This cannot be changed after a user flow has been created.

* B2C_1_ | signup_signin | ✓

Figure 2-40. *User flow name*

9. As shown in Figure 2-41, you can define the identity
    providers, and you should select at least one
    here. So we will be selecting the default one for
    this example. Also, you could define multifactor
    authentication here, but let's leave it disabled for
    this example.

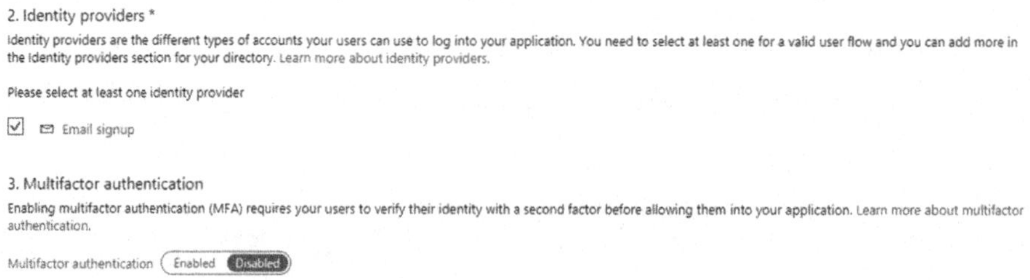

2. Identity providers *
Identity providers are the different types of accounts your users can use to log into your application. You need to select at least one for a valid user flow and you can add more in
the Identity providers section for your directory. Learn more about identity providers.

Please select at least one identity provider

☑   ✉ Email signup

3. Multifactor authentication
Enabling multifactor authentication (MFA) requires your users to verify their identity with a second factor before allowing them into your application. Learn more about multifactor
authentication.

Multifactor authentication   (Enabled **Disabled**)

Figure 2-41. *Defining identity providers*

10. The next step is to define the user attributes and
     claims that are collected during sign-up. By default
     on this screen, only a few fields are defined. Click
     the "Show more" link to add more fields. After
     selecting the fields required, then click the Ok
     button (Figure 2-42).

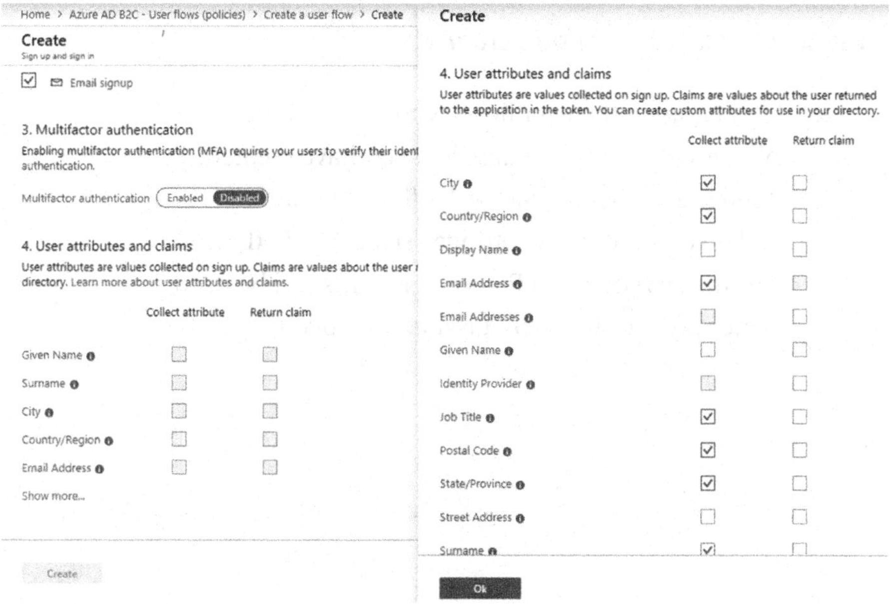

Figure 2-42. *User attributes and claims*

11. Finally, click the Create button at the bottom of the
     screen to complete the process, and the new user
     flow will be created. Similarly, create the user flow
     for Profile Editing and Password Reset. As shown in
     Figure 2-43, all flows you have created will be listed.

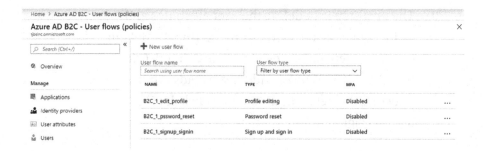

Figure 2-43. List of user flows created

12. After creating the user flows, you must set the
     following settings for each flow you have created.
     Open the Properties tab of the flow and under
     "Token compatibility settings," select the URL with
     the /tfp/, as shown in Figure 2-44. This will be used
     to identify the claims that issued the token.

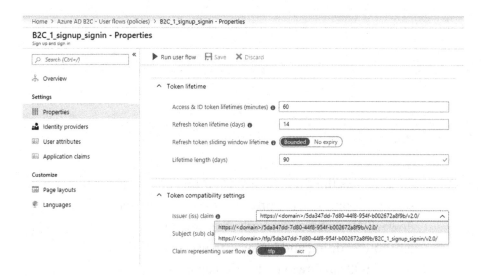

Figure 2-44. User flow properties

Perform this action for the other flows you have created. There are other properties on this form, and you can configure them as per the requirements.

Portal Configuration

Now that you have configured Azure AD B2C, the next step is to configure the portal to federate with Azure AD B2C using the Open ID Connect protocol.

1. Sign into the Dynamics 365 portal app and open Site Settings. Create the following entries:

Name	Value
Authenticationn/OpenIdConnect/ B2C/Authority	<The issuer URL>
Authentication/OpenIdConnect/ B2C/ClientId	2f9237da-553f-41b0-a79f-374e83ba8b28
Authentication/OpenIdConnect/ B2C/RedirectUri	`https://sbmamember.microsoftcrm portals.com/signin-b2`

2. To support the federated sign-out, create the following entry in Site Settings:

Name	Value
Authentication/OpenIdConnection /B2C/ExternalLogoutEnabled	true

3. Create the following entry to hard-code the portal to a single identity provider:

Name	Value
Authentication/OpenIdConnection/B2C/ LoginButtonAuthenticationType	\<Policy sign in URL\>

4. Configure the password reset and create the following entries:

Name	Value
Authentication/OpenIdConnect/B2C/ PasswordResetPolicyId	\<ID of password reset policy\>
Authentication/OpenIdConnect/B2C/ ValidIssuers	\<A comma-separated list of issuers that includes the policy sign-in URL and the issuer\>
Authentication/OpenIdConnect/B2C/ DefaultPolicyId	\<ID of the sign-in/sign-up policy\>

5. To support the claims mapping, enter the following entries:

Name	Value
Authentication/ OpenIdConnect/ B2C/Registration ClaimsMapping	emailaddress1=http://schemas.xmlsoap. org/ws/2005/05/identity/claims/ emailaddress,firstname=http://schemas.xmlsoap. org/ws/2005/05/identity/claims/givenname,last name=http://schemas.xmlsoap.org/ws/2005/05/ identity/claims/surname

6.   Then enter the caption of the button:

Name	Value
Authentication/OpenIdConnect/B2C/Caption	Azure AD B2C

For more settings such as related site settings, related content snippets, etc., please visit https://docs.microsoft.com/en-us/dynamics365/ customer-engagement/portals/azure-ad-b2c#portal-configuration.

Figure 2-45 illustrates the list of values entered into Site Settings.

𝄢 Active Site Settings ⌄

✓	Name	↑ ▽	Value	▽	Website
	Authentication/OpenIdConnect/Azure AD B2C/AllowContactMappingWithEmail		true		Custom Portal
	Authentication/OpenIdConnect/Azure AD B2C/LoginClaimsMapping		true		Custom Portal
	Authentication/OpenIdConnect/B2C/Authority		https://login.microsoftonline.com/tfp/30da4020-68e4-4530-ac7a-a0f8aecb0cc2/b...		Custom Portal
	Authentication/OpenIdConnect/B2C/Caption		Azure AD B2C		Custom Portal
	Authentication/OpenIdConnect/B2C/ClientId		8075a5ce-2538-4bd4-b61d-1e9349ad923e		Custom Portal
	Authentication/OpenIdConnect/B2C/ExternalLogoutEnabled		true		Custom Portal
	Authentication/OpenIdConnect/B2C/RedirectUrl		https://contoso.microsoftcrmportals.com/signin-b2c		Custom Portal
	Authentication/OpenIdConnect/B2C/RegistrationClaimsMapping		emailaddress1=http://schemas.xmlsoap.org/ws/2005/05/identity/claims/emailad...		Custom Portal

Figure 2-45. *Azure B2C Site Settings*

Let's do a quick test to see whether it navigates to the Azure AD B2C login page. As shown in Figure 2-46, click the Azure AD B2C button.

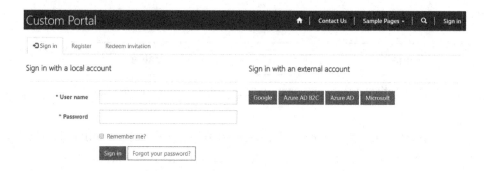

Figure 2-46. *Sign-in page, Azure AD B2C*

If you have set up the configuration correctly, then you will be directed to the default login screen, as shown in Figure 2-47.

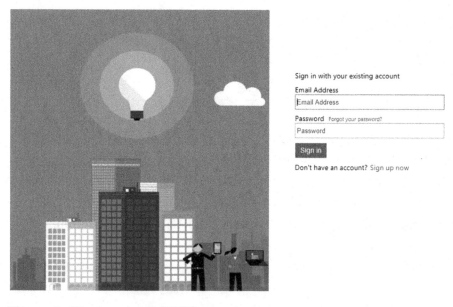

Figure 2-47. *Azure AD B2C login screen*

User Authorization

No matter what authentication technique is used in your portal, once a user is authenticated, you should authorize the user. This means you are giving authorization to perform certain tasks on the portal. First, let's look at web roles, which are the cornerstone for authorizing the contacts.

Web Roles

After authenticating the contacts, every contact must be granted a web role. By default, when you configure the portal, you will get three web roles that are considered the most commonly used. Navigate to Web Roles under the Security section in the left navigation pane (Figure 2-48).

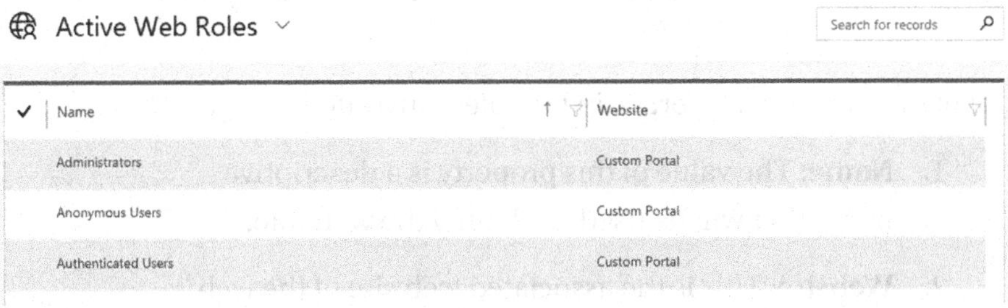

Figure 2-48. *Active web roles*

As shown in Figure 2-43, there are three web roles that were created: Administrator, Anonymous Users, and Authenticated Users (these roles were briefly described at the beginning of this chapter). To dig deep into these roles, let's open the Anonymous Users and Authenticated Users roles (Figure 2-49).

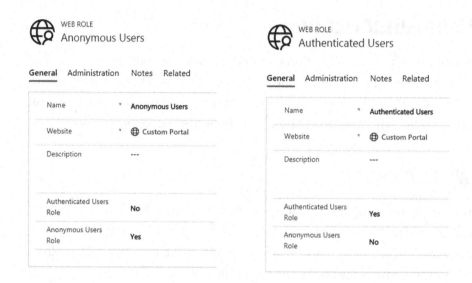

Figure 2-49. *Anonymous Users and Authenticated Users web roles*

Let's look at the properties in the roles illustrated in Figure 2-49.

1. **Name**: The value of this property is a descriptive name that will be used to identify the web role.

2. **Website**: This is the associated web site of the web role.

3. **Description**: This is an optional field that can be filled only if you want to add more detail about the role.

4. **Authenticated User Role**: This is a Boolean value, and if set to true, then the role will be the default for authenticated users. There can be only one web role with this setting set to true. This will be the default web role for authenticated users who have not been assigned a web role.

5. **Anonymous User Role**: This also a Boolean value, and if set to true, then the role will be the default for unauthenticated users. There can be only one web role with this setting set to true, and it will be the default web role for unauthenticated users. This will solely adhere to the entity permissions.

The administrator permission is the superuser for the portal, and by default, the role cannot do much. Therefore, you should edit this role to make it a proper Administrator role. In addition to these, you can create other web roles as per your requirements. The next level of web roles is the entity permissions, which will determine the record-level access of the authenticated users.

Entity Permissions

The entity permissions are used to grant record-level permissions to authenticated users. Once the entity permissions are created, they can be associated with the web roles. You should keep in mind that an authenticated portal user can have multiple roles, and a given web role will have multiple entity permissions. As a best practice, when you design the portal, you should consider determining the web roles and entity permissions. You can create the entity permissions under the entity permissions and add them to the web roles. For instance, the example of this book uses event management. Let's assume we want to provide entity permission to administrators for the Event entity.

Navigate to Entity Permissions and click New. Fill in the required information and select the entity from the drop-down list on the right side of the screen (Figure 2-50).

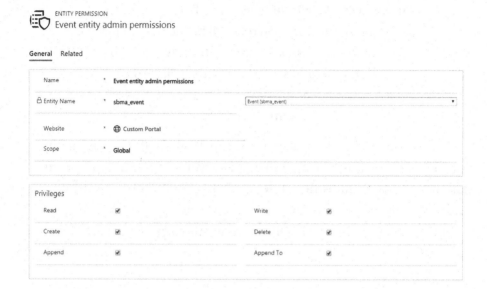

Figure 2-50. *Event entity permissions*

The other important thing when creating the entity permissions is the scope, which determines whether the user has access to all the records. For instance, as per this example, if the global scope is defined, then the web role that this permission is assigned to will have access to all the records in the system.

- **Global scope:** If a contact is assigned the web role, which is assigned with an entity permission with a Global scope, then the contact will have access to all the records in the given entity. For more information, visit https://docs.microsoft.com/en-us/ dynamics365/customer-engagement/portals/assign- entity-permissions#global-scope.

- **Contact scope:** If a contact is assigned a web role that has an entity permission with a Contact scope, then the user will only have access to the records associated with that contact of the user. This means the records will be filtered by the current user. For more information, visit https://docs.microsoft.com/en-us/dynamics365/customer-engagement/portals/assign-entity-permissions#contact-scope.

- **Account scope**: This scope will allow the users (contacts) to access the records within the same account. For more information, visit https://docs.microsoft.com/en-us/dynamics365/customer-engagement/portals/assign-entity-permissions#account-scope.

- **Self scope**: This is to make changes to their own contact record such as the default access a user has to the profile page. But if the user requires access to any custom entity forms or web forms, then they will require this permission. For more information, visit https://docs.microsoft.com/en-us/dynamics365/customer-engagement/portals/assign-entity-permissions#self-scope.

- **Parent scope**: This is the most complex of all the scopes described. When this scope is applied, it means the privileges to the entity record are granted through the parent-child relationship chain. For more information, visit https://docs.microsoft.com/en-us/dynamics365/customer-engagement/portals/assign-entity-permissions#parental-scope. A nice example is given here that can be used with the Dynamics 365 portals: https://community.adxstudio.com/products/adxstudio-portals/documentation/configuration-guide/entity-permissions/attributes-and-relationships/

In our example, we will be giving full access to the event records for those users who have the Event Administrator role. This Event Administrator role will be associated with the Event entity admin permission that was created earlier. The next step is to create the child permissions to related record. The requirement is that the Event Administrators should have access to all the events, event registrations, payments, and other event planning details.

Navigate to the entity permission created, scroll down to the subgrid that lists the child permissions, and click the +Add New Entity Permission button on the command bar (Figure 2-51).

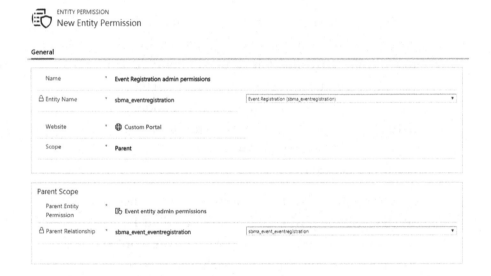

Figure 2-51. *Child entity permission settings*

Enter all the required information and select Parent as the scope; you will notice a new section appears so you can enter the relationship details. This implies that the event administrator will have full control over the event registration of a given event.

Important   For these permissions to work, you must enable entity permissions on the entity lists and entity forms. See Figure 2-52 and Figure 2-53. Furthermore, the child or the related entity must have a subgrid on the parent form. That is, the event form should list all the related event registrations that the user can click and open. In addition, you should also configure the Event Registration entity forms with create and edit permissions. In the next chapter, this book will demonstrate the actual usage of this permission when configuring and editing lists and forms.

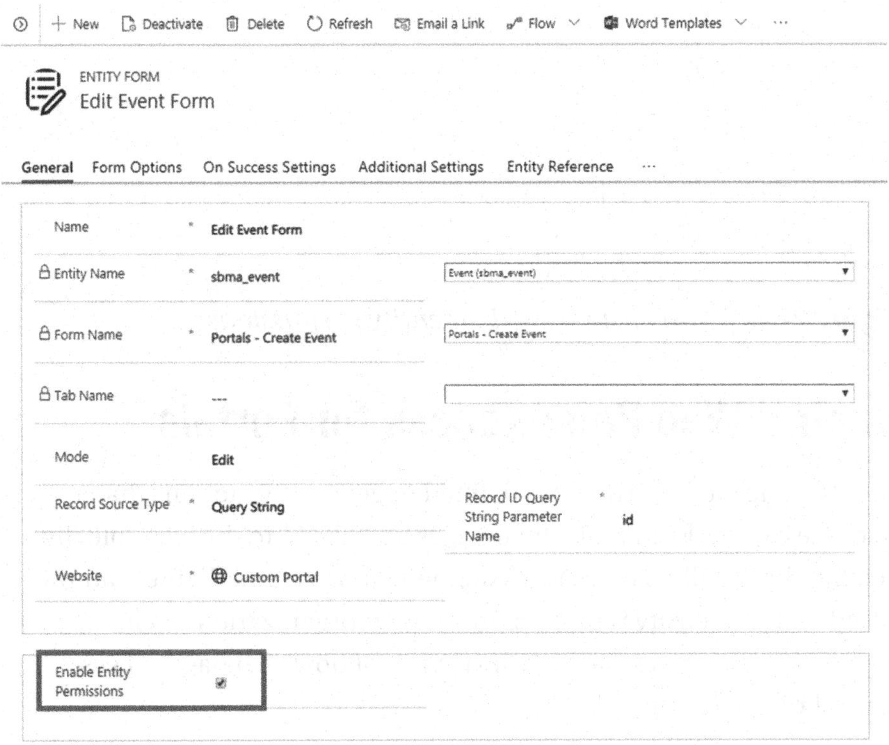

Figure 2-52. *Entity form enabled for entity permissions*

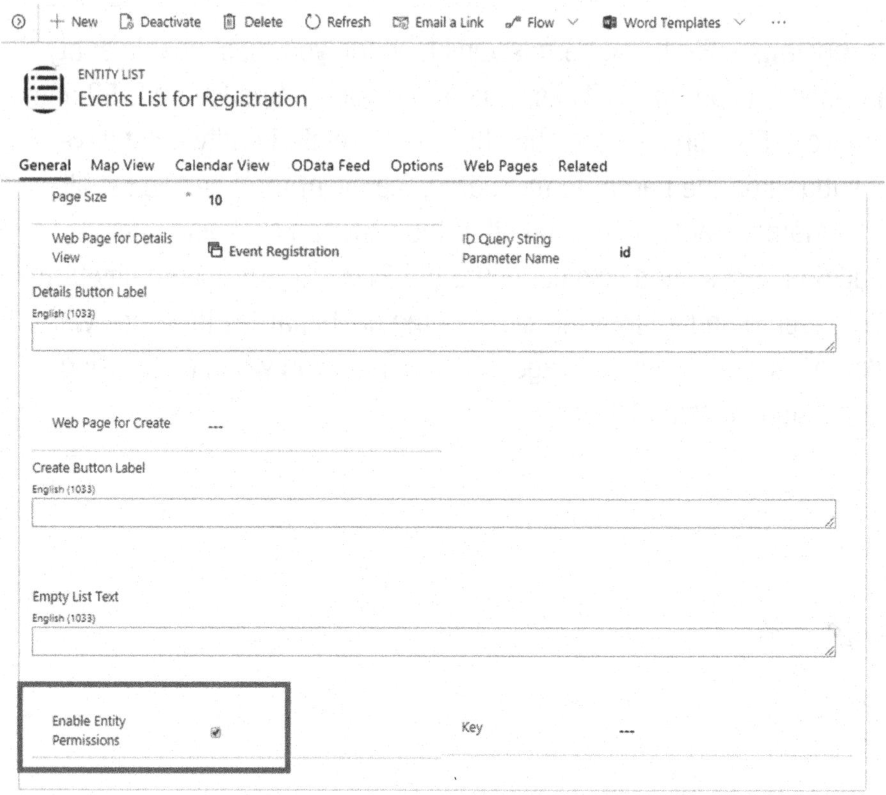

Figure 2-53. *Entity list enabled for entity permissions*

Control Web Page Access for Portals

The web page access rules are defined to govern the actions that a web role can perform and which pages are visible to the web role. By default, there will be three rules defined, and you can define your own based on the security requirements of your organization or client. Figure 2-54 illustrates the high-level view of how web page access control rules are applied.

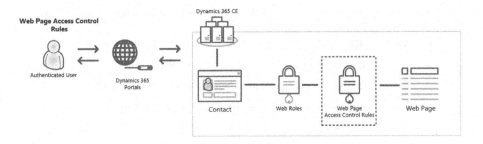

Figure 2-54. *Web page access control rules*

When you navigate to Security and then "Web page access control rules," you can see the list of access control rules in the current configuration. Also, every web page has an Access Control Rule tab that lists all the access control rules associated with the current page. Figure 2-55 illustrates the list of properties of the access control rules.

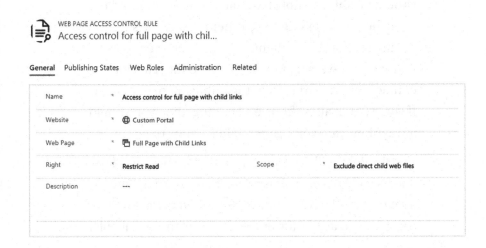

Figure 2-55. *Web page access rules*

There are few important properties you should understand on this form.

- **Web Page**: This is the page the rules will apply to, and it will be applied to all the child pages of this page. So, you must be extra careful because if you select the home page, the rule will be applied to all the pages within the portal.

- **Right**: There are two options available: Grant Change and Restrict Read.

  Grant Change enables the user in the web role linked with the rule to publish content changes to both the current page and its child pages. Grant Change will take precedence over a restricted read. For instance, within a given event details page, the event organizer should be able to publish updates, but they should not have the full access rights to other parts of the site. You should set the Grant Change right on the event page and assign the associating web role to the relevant contact/user, making them the publisher of this event. If you want to allow front-end editing, then you should always look into setting up Grant Change rules.

  Restrict Read will limit specific users from viewing a page and its child pages. This is a restrictive rule that limits a set of users. For instance, you might want the event organizers to access the event section of the portal only.

- **Scope**: This property will have two option. "All content" means the security validations will be enforced on all the child content. "Exclude direct child web files" will ignore child web content directly related to the current web page from the security validations. The default value is "All content."

How this works is bit tricky. Let's assume a scenario where you have four web pages: wp1, wp2, wp3, and wp4. If you want to give access to wp1 and wp2 to the anonymous user, restrict wp3 and wp4 using an authenticated web role for the access control rule. The logged-in/authenticated users can see wp3 and wp4, and the anonymous users can see wp1 and wp2 but not wp3 and wp4. If the anonymous user clicks the wp3 or wp4 link, they will be directed to the sign-in page.

Create Web Site Access Permissions

These permissions will permit the users to edit the elements of the portal other than the web pages. The settings will determine which components will be managed in the portal. By default, there are two such rules created. See Figure 2-56.

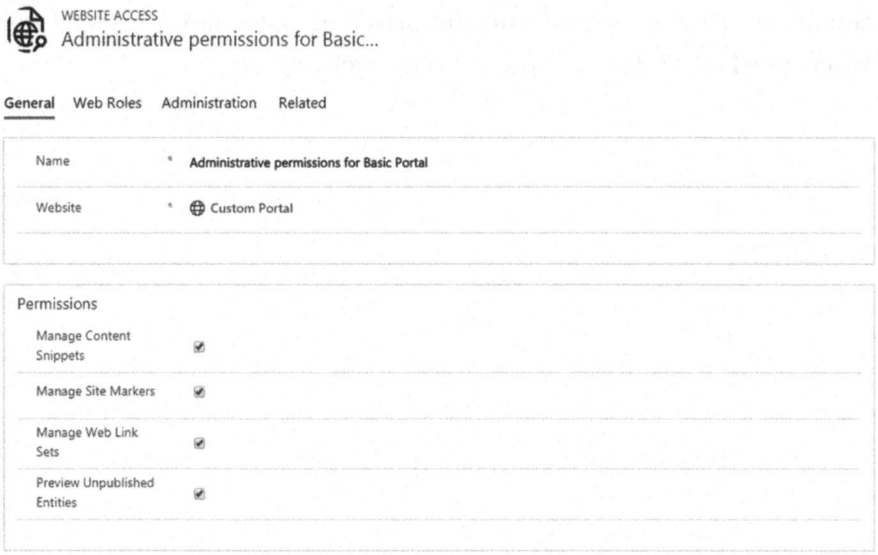

Figure 2-56. Web site access permissions

Under the Permissions section, the following settings are available:

- Manage Content Snippets allows modifications to the snippet control.

- Manage Site Markers permits modifications to the hyperlinks that use the site markers.

- Manage Weblink Sets permits adding and removing links from the web link sets.

- Preview Unpublished Entities allows users to view the portal-enabled entities in draft mode.

As shown in Figure 2-56, you can specify the web roles for this rule on the Web Roles tab.

Summary

With that, I have covered most of the important security aspects of portals including both authentication and authorization. In the next chapter, I will demonstrate how to display content on the web pages.

CHAPTER 3

Data Entry and Customization

In the previous chapter, I discussed the security aspects of Dynamics 365 portals and how to configure them. In this chapter, the main focus is on customizing the portal further to meet the requirements of the example scenario. Initially, the chapter will show how to customize the pages and add a few pages required for the application. Then, it will guide you through creating entity forms, creating entity lists, and displaying charts on your portal.

Customizing the Portal

In this section, you'll change the text on the pages, change the banner images, and add a few new pages to meet the requirements.

Changing the Banner Text

When you log in as the system administrator, you will see the content editor; currently, there is a new editor available in preview mode. A message bar will be displayed on the top with a "Try new editor" button (Figure 3-1).

© Sanjaya Yapa 2019
S. Yapa, *Getting Started with Dynamics 365 Portals*,
https://doi.org/10.1007/978-1-4842-5346-5_3

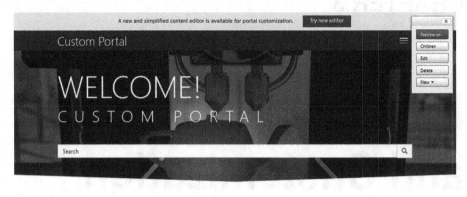

Figure 3-1. *Admin login with editors enabled*

First, let's change the banner text. Just hover over the banner text and the Edit button appears (Figure 3-2). Click the Edit button and the editor window pops up. Enter the text you want to use and click Save, and the text will be changed accordingly. Similarly, change the other text on the banner. As soon as you save the changes in the respective editor, the changes will be applied to the page.

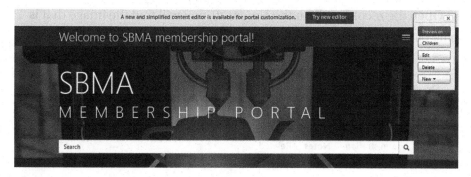

Figure 3-2. *Banner text changed*

Changing the Banner Image

Let's change the banner image. In the portal app, navigate to the web files and look for the record named homehero.jpg (Figure 3-3).

Figure 3-3. *Active web files, banner image*

Open the record, and on the Notes tab, you will find the image that is being used. Add a new note with a new image attached (Figure 3-4).

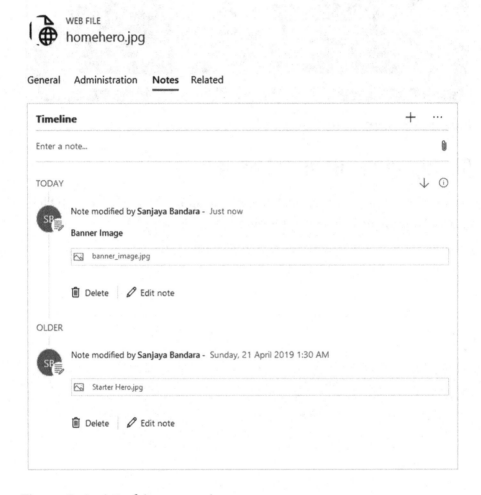

Figure 3-4. *Attaching a new image*

Navigate back to the portal, and in the content editor window, select Children. Find the homehero.jpg file and click the edit icon (Figure 3-5).

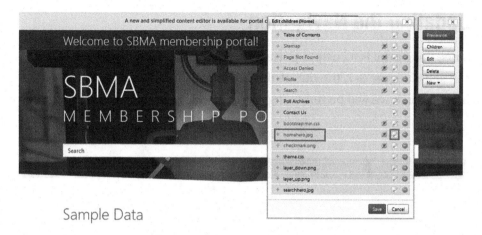

Figure 3-5. *Changing the banner, edit icon*

The "Edit this file" window will pop up. Click the browse button, select the image from the file location, upload the file, and click the Save button at the bottom-right corner of the window. Click Save in the editor, and the browser will automatically refresh and load the page with the new image, as shown in Figure 3-6.

Figure 3-6. *Portal banner after changing the banner image*

Updating the Navigation

Since this portal is a custom portal, the navigation must be edited. As you can see in Figure 3-7, the out-of-the-box navigation contains a few sample pages, which we will be removing. We will add the pages we require to the navigation.

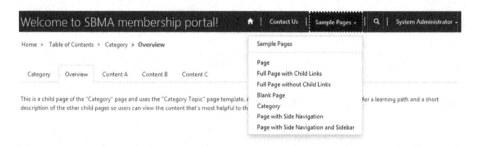

Figure 3-7. *Default navigation and sample pages*

To update the primary navigation, hover the mouse pointer over the primary navigation, and you will see the Edit button appear at the top of the navigation (Figure 3-8). Then the Edit Primary Navigation editor will appear, and you can add new pages, add existing pages to the navigation, remove unwanted pages, and change the position of the links.

Figure 3-8. *Editing the primary navigation*

Click the green add icon at the bottom of the editor, and you will be directed to a screen where you can enter the details of the page. As you can see in Figure 3-9, you can select the page you want to display from the Page drop-down button. This drop-down list will display all the pages available, so you can select the required one. If the page you want to display is an external page, then you can specify the URL of the external page.

Note that the publishing state is to define whether the link is published or not. The final four properties are all related to link images. For instance, if you want to display an image instead of text, you can specify the URL of the image and other properties such as width, height, and alternate text of the image.

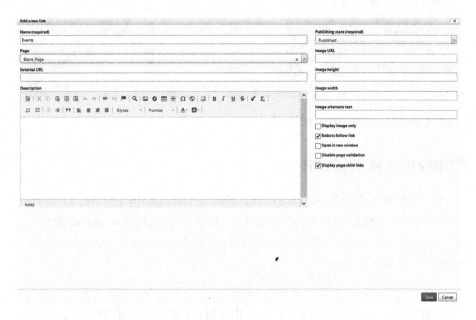

Figure 3-9. *Adding a new link form*

Once you click the Save button, notice that the new page will appear in the Edit Primary Navigation editor. Click the Save button in the editor to confirm the addition of the new link. You can now see that the navigation has been edited per your requirements (Figure 3-10).

Figure 3-10. *Updated navigation*

To add a child page, make sure that you deselect the "Display page child links" checkbox in the "Add new link" form and click Save. In the editor, drag the child page under the parent page, as illustrated in Figure 3-11.

Figure 3-11. *Inserting a child*

Applying a Theme

Most of the time developers are compelled to change the theme of a portal to enforce the branding of the business. There are many themes available, but to keep things simple, this book will guide you in applying a simple theme from Bootswatch.

Important   At the time of writing this book, the out-of-the-box theme of Dynamics 365 portals is based on Bootstrap version 3 from Bootswatch. So, you should download the Bootstrap theme from https://bootswatch.com/3/.

When you open the Bootswatch page, there are several free themes that you can download. First, download your preferred theme. As shown in Figure 3-12, click the "Child file" option.

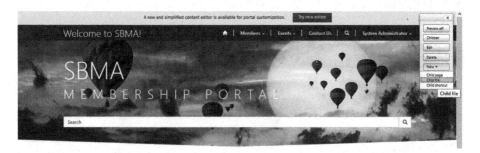

Figure 3-12. *Creating a new child file for the theme CSS file*

This action will open the "Create a new child file" form where you should enter the details of the theme file (Figure 3-13). After adding the information, hit the Save button, which will create a web file in Dynamics 365 CE portal admin application with the CSS file as an attachment to the notes.

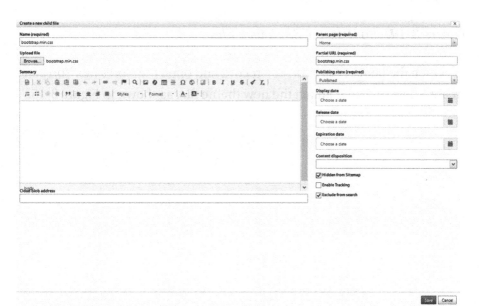

Figure 3-13. *Applying a theme*

Make sure that you enter the Name as "bootstrap.min.css" and copy the same to the Partial URL field as seen in Figure 3-13.

If you go to the web files, you can see the `bootstrap.min.css` file is listed (Figure 3-14).

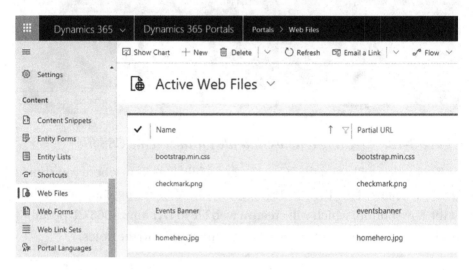

Figure 3-14. *Bootstrap CSS in web files*

Open the `bootstrap.min.css` record and open the Notes tab. You can create a new note and attach the new theme file, as shown in Figure 3-15.

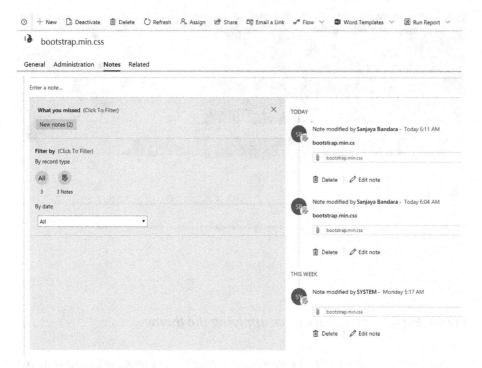

Figure 3-15. *Bootstrap CSS attached to notes*

Once the changes have been applied, you can refresh the portal to
see the changes. Sometimes changes might not be visible with a simple
refresh. In such situations, navigate to the portal Admin Center and
open Portal Actions. Click Restart, and the new theme will be applied
(Figure 3-16).

Sample Data

This portal uses sample data for illustration purposes.

The starter portal is a basic portal that provides you with content, templates, and infrastructure to help you get started and build a functional portal for your organization quickly and efficiently.

With this solution you get access to the following:

- Branding and personalization
- Sign-in and registration
- Profile management
- Content templates that you can apply to any of your pages
- Ads and polls

Figure 3-16. *Home page after applying the theme*

You can see the changes more clearly when you navigate to the sign-in page (Figure 3-17).

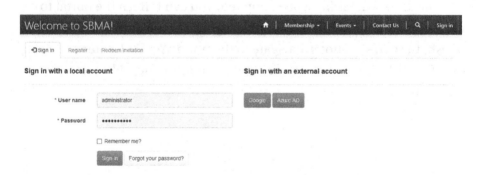

Figure 3-17. *Sign-in page after applying the new theme*

Adding Pages and Customizing Pages

To create a web page, go to the Web Pages option in the Content section of the right pane. Then click the +New button to create the new page (Figure 3-18). At this level, we will just be creating a placeholder. Later in this chapter, we will be adding a list to show the available events created in the system.

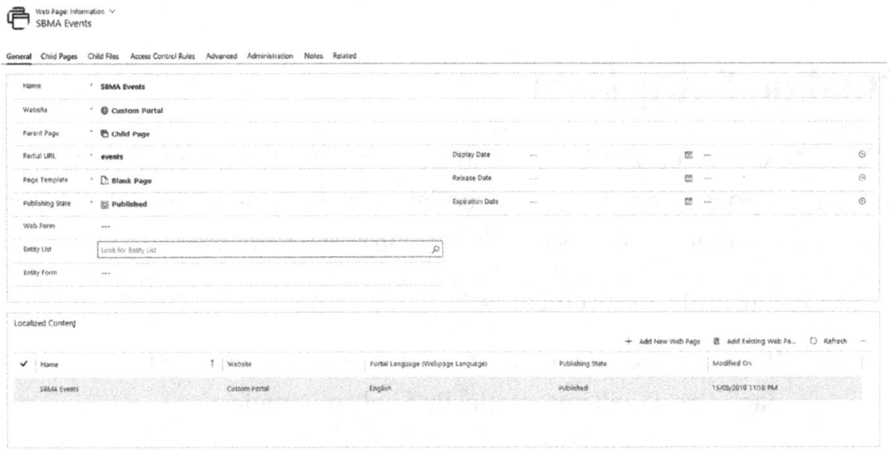

Figure 3-18. *Creating a new page*

As you can see, you should provide some important information on this form. The full description of each of these attributes can be found at https://docs.microsoft.com/en-us/dynamics365/customer-engagement/portals/web-page#web-page-attributes. Let's quickly add this page to the navigation.

As previously explained, open the navigation editor and change the page to the new page you created; save the changes (Figure 3-19). As a best practice, you should first create the pages you want and update the navigation accordingly. Next, we will look at adding an entity list to the web page and loading some data. As of now, the page that you created is a blank page.

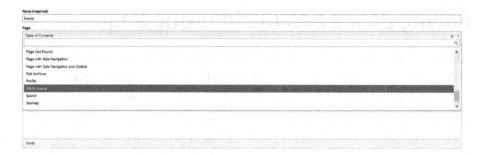

Figure 3-19. *Changing the page*

Creating Entity Lists

Entity lists are used to render the list of records stored in a Dynamics 365 CE entity. Even power users can easily configure an entity list without developer help. The grid that lists the records is capable of the following:

- The grid can sort records.

- If the number of records exceeds the page's specified page size, it will automatically apply pagination.

- The entity list also supports multiple views in a scenario where multiple views have been specified.

- If you have specified a web page for a detailed view, then each record will contain a link to the details page. When you click the link, the record ID will be appended to the query string to load the details page.

- Also, records can be filtered if values exist for the Portal User and Account attributes. The grid will render a drop-down list to facilitate the filtering.

The most important thing to remember is that an entity list must be associated with a web page for the list to be visible on the portal. To create the entity list, under the Content section of the right pane, click the Entity Lists option. Click +New to create a new entity list (Figure 3-20). After adding the primary information, click Save. There are many other properties available on this form, and as you can see, there are multiple views specified to view both active and inactive events. For a full list of attributes and relationships, please visit `https://docs.microsoft.com/en-us/dynamics365/customer-engagement/portals/add-webpage-render-list-records#entity-list-attributes-and-relationships`.

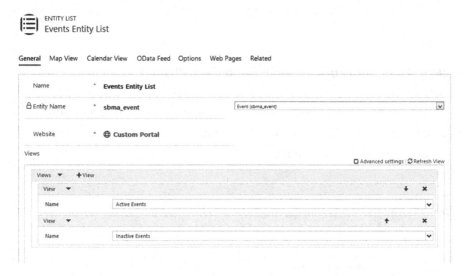

Figure 3-20. *Creating an entity list*

Now that we have created a simple entity list, let's add it to the web page created. As shown in Figure 3-21, add the entity list and save it.

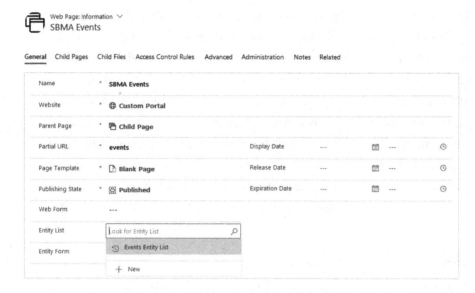

Figure 3-21. *Adding the entity list to the web page*

After saving these changes to the web page, add the access control rules for the web page (Figure 3-22). In Chapter 2, we created a rule specific to events management.

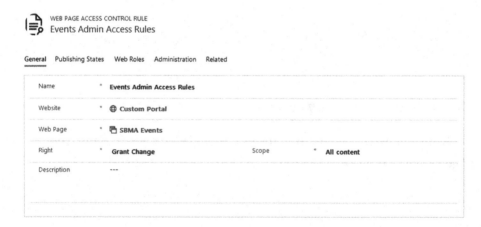

Figure 3-22. *Web page access control rule for events page*

Make sure the relevant web roles are added to the access rule as well. Also in Chapter 2, we created the entity permissions, which will determine what the user can do with the records. Once all these settings are configured, navigate to the new page, and you can see the list of events created in the Dynamics 365 CE being displayed in the portal (Figure 3-23).

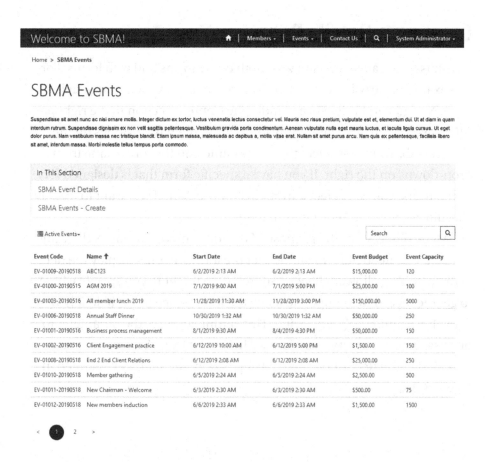

Figure 3-23. Event entity list displayed on a web page

Note   As explained earlier, you can see that the entity list has pagination and sorting enabled on it.

Next, let's create a details page.

Creating a Details Page

A details page can be created with both entity forms and web forms. For this example, we will create an entity form to display the event details page. Navigate to Entity Forms under the Content section in the right pane. Click +New to create a new entity form. Enter the basic settings on the General tab. You must select the entity name and the form name from the drop-downs on the right. If you have a specific form that is designed for portal users, you can select it from this drop-down. If you want to display a specific tab, you can select it from there.

Mode determines the purpose of the form. In this example, the value selected was ReadOnly, meaning that the form will only display the details, with no editing allowed. Record Source Type is where you specify where to get the record to manipulate using the form. Since this is a details view, the value should be Query String. This setting requires the parameter to be passed via the query string of the URL to the form. This parameter is specified in the Record ID Query String Parameter field, as illustrated in Figure 3-24.

ENTITY FORM
New Entity Form

General   Form Options   On Success Settings   Additional Settings   Entity Reference   Entity Form Metadata

Name	* **Event Details**	
🔒 Entity Name	* **sbma_event**	Event (sbma_event)
🔒 Form Name	* **Information**	Information
🔒 Tab Name	---	
Mode	**ReadOnly**	
Record Source Type *	**Query String**	Record ID Query * String Parameter **id** Name
Website	* ⊕ **Custom Portal**	

Enable Entity Permissions	☑

Figure 3-24. Entity form settings

For a full list of settings, please follow this link: `https://docs.`
`microsoft.com/en-us/dynamics365/customer-engagement/portals/`
`entity-forms-custom-logic#entity-form-attributes-and-`
`relationships`. Save the settings; now you should create the web page to
host the entity form you have just created.

Note   You must select the SBMA events and the parent page that
has the event entity list.

Save the settings, open the entity list, and scroll down to the property
Web Page for Details View. Select the web page you have just created
(Figure 3-25).

Web Page for Details View	🗐 SBMA Event Details	ID Query String Parameter Name	id

Figure 3-25. *Setting web page to display the data*

Save the changes and refresh the portal site. You can see, the field Event Code is highlighted in blue, meaning that it is a hyperlink to open the details about each event record (see Figure 3-26).

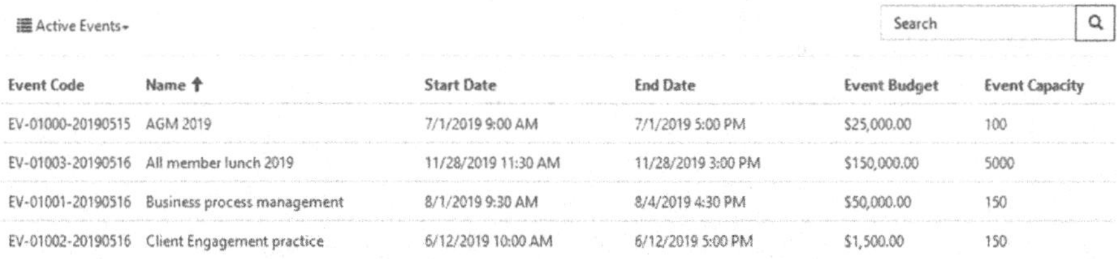

Active Events▾				Search	🔍
Event Code	**Name ✝**	**Start Date**	**End Date**	**Event Budget**	**Event Capacity**
EV-01000-20190515	AGM 2019	7/1/2019 9:00 AM	7/1/2019 5:00 PM	$25,000.00	100
EV-01003-20190516	All member lunch 2019	11/28/2019 11:30 AM	11/28/2019 3:00 PM	$150,000.00	5000
EV-01001-20190516	Business process management	8/1/2019 9:30 AM	8/4/2019 4:30 PM	$50,000.00	150
EV-01002-20190516	Client Engagement practice	6/12/2019 10:00 AM	6/12/2019 5:00 PM	$1,500.00	150

Figure 3-26. *Entity list after mapping the details form*

When you click the link, it will take you to the details page. The most important thing to remember here is that since you have set this form as a view-only form, if your form has any field with editable fields, those fields will not be visible on this form. For instance, if you have selected one of the main information forms in CRM and if the fields are read-write, then none of the fields will be displayed. Therefore, you must create another form in the CRM system with read-only fields and select that form in the entity form settings. As shown in Figure 3-27, the fields of the Dynamics 365 CE form is read-only.

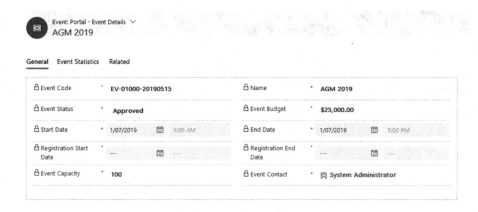

Figure 3-27. *Dynamics 365 forms with read-only fields*

When you open the details page in the portal, you can see the fields are read-only as well (Figure 3-28).

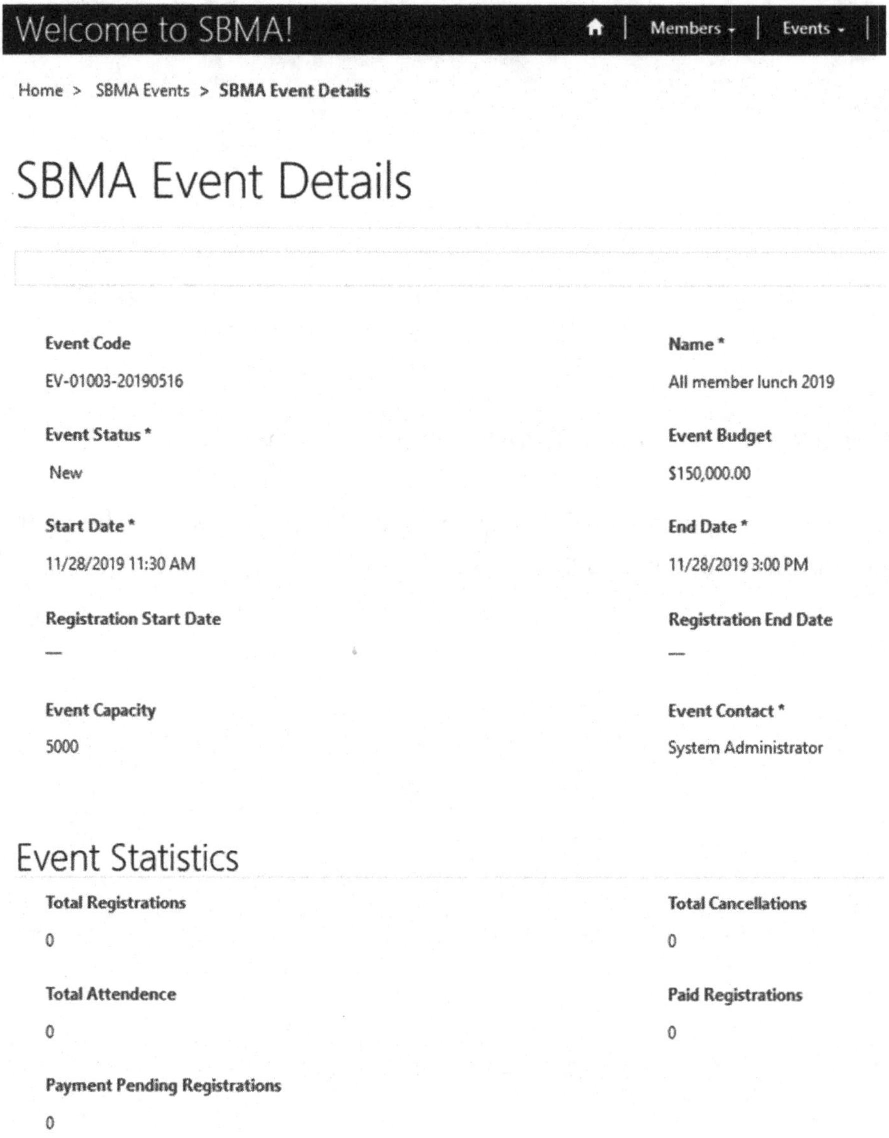
Welcome to SBMA!
Members
Events
Home > SBMA Events > SBMA Event Details
SBMA Event Details
Event Code
EV-01003-20190516
Name *
All member lunch 2019
Event Status *
New
Event Budget
$150,000.00
Start Date *
11/28/2019 11:30 AM
End Date *
11/28/2019 3:00 PM
Registration Start Date
—
Registration End Date
—
Event Capacity
5000
Event Contact *
System Administrator
Event Statistics
Total Registrations
0
Total Cancellations
0
Total Attendence
0
Paid Registrations
0
Payment Pending Registrations
0

Figure 3-28. *Event details page*

Creating a Form

Similar to creating the details page, a create form can be configured with entity forms. Unlike the details form, you must select the mode as Insert, which indicates this entity form is for creating or inserting new records. So, as the first step, create the entity form and provide the required information, as shown in Figure 3-29.

ENTITY FORM
Create Event Form

General   Form Options   On Success Settings   Additional Settings   Entity Reference   ⋯

Name	*	**Create Event Form**	
🔒 Entity Name	*	**sbma_event**	Event (sbma_event) ▾
🔒 Form Name	*	**Portals - Create Event**	Portals - Create Event ▾
🔒 Tab Name		---	▾
Mode		**Insert**	
Website	*	⊕ **Custom Portal**	

Figure 3-29. *Creating the event form's general settings*

Save the settings. One extra step that you should do per the requirements is to associate the event you create with the current user. Open the Entity References tab and select Yes from the Set Entity Reference On Save drop-down list (Figure 3-30). More details about the properties can be found at `https://docs.microsoft.com/en-us/dynamics365/customer-engagement/portals/entity-forms-custom-logic#entity-reference`.

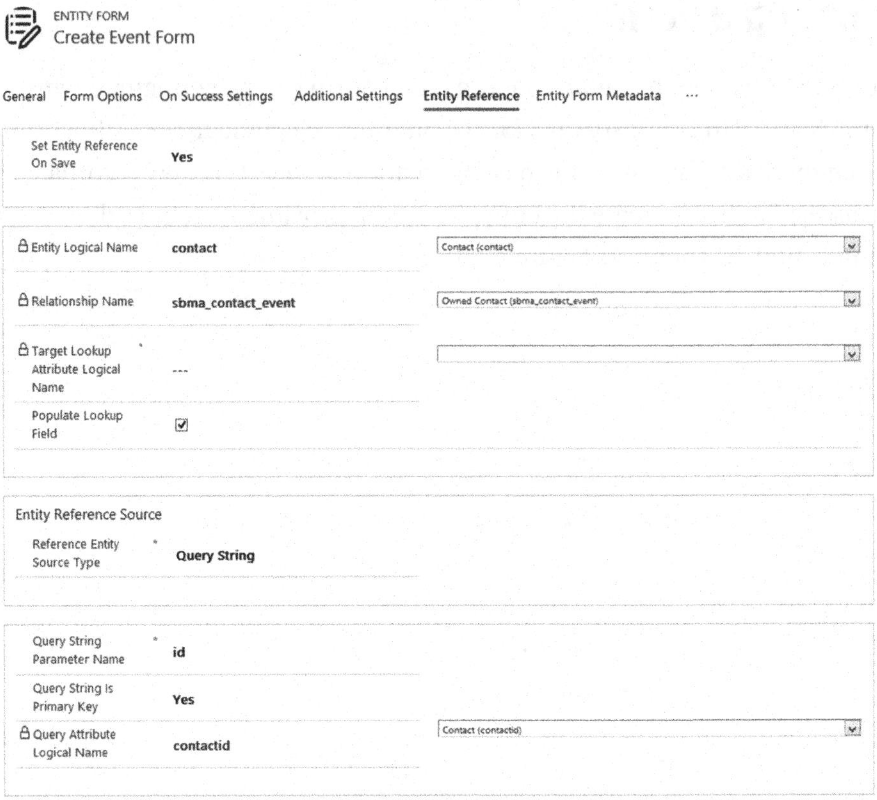

ENTITY FORM
Create Event Form

General   Form Options   On Success Settings   Additional Settings   **Entity Reference**   Entity Form Metadata   ...

Set Entity Reference On Save	**Yes**	

🔒 Entity Logical Name	**contact**	Contact (contact) ▾
🔒 Relationship Name	**sbma_contact_event**	Owned Contact (sbma_contact_event) ▾
🔒 Target Lookup Attribute Logical Name	---	▾
Populate Lookup Field	☑	

Entity Reference Source

Reference Entity Source Type	**Query String**

Query String Parameter Name	**id**	
Query String Is Primary Key	**Yes**	
🔒 Query Attribute Logical Name	**contactid**	Contact (contactid) ▾

Figure 3-30. *Entity reference settings*

Next, go to the Event Entity List record, and on the Options tab, scroll down to the Grid Configuration section of the form (Figure 3-31). This will allow you to define the view actions. Click +Create and select the entity form that you created in the previous step.

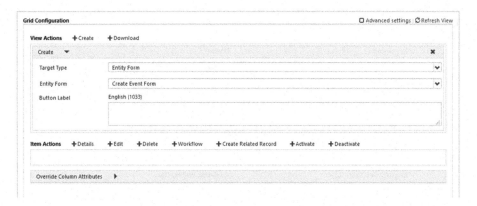

Figure 3-31. *Grid configuration, Create button*

Save the settings and navigate to the Events list, and you can see that the new +Create button appears on top of the view, as shown in Figure 3-32.

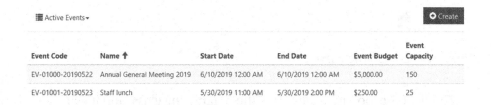

Figure 3-32. *Create button on the view*

Click the button, and a new pop-up window will appear to enter the event details (Figure 3-33).

Note   As you may have noticed, this create event form is not associated with a web page. This is simply because the form is associated with the view.

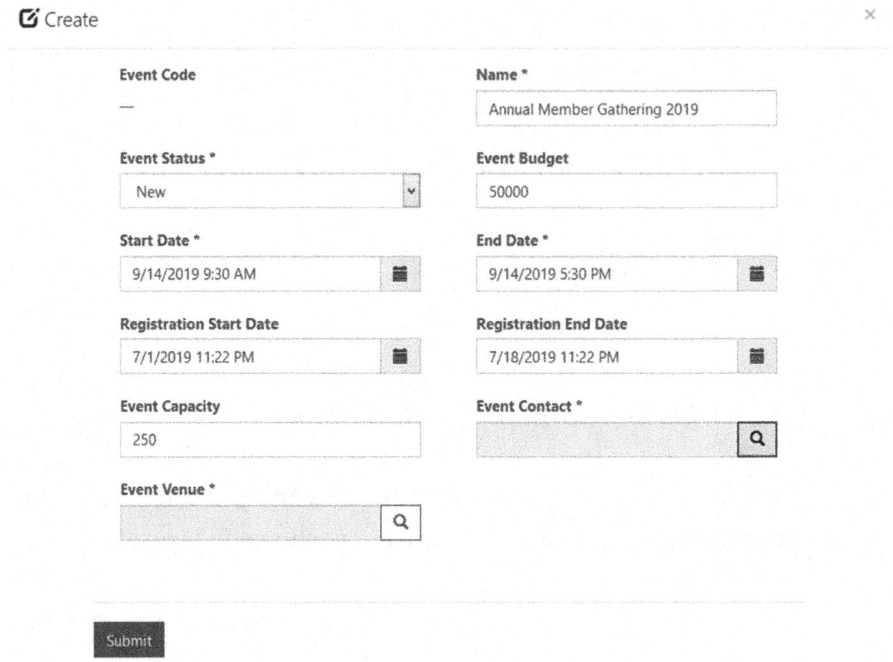

Figure 3-33. *Create form*

To select the lookup values, click the magnifying glass, and it will display the lookup selector, as shown in Figure 3-34.

Figure 3-34. *Lookup value selection window*

Editing a Form

Similar to creating the create record form, we can create a new entity form and set the required settings as per our requirements. Select Edit from the Mode property, as shown in Figure 3-35.

Note   In Figure 3-35, you can see that the Portals – Create Event form is selected. You have the option to create a specific form just for editing by exposing only the fields that can be edited by the portal users. Also, if you are setting the entity references, you must make sure the user has the appropriate entity permissions (Read, Append, and Append To). Otherwise, the user will not be able to edit or create the record since the users do not have permission for the referencing entity.

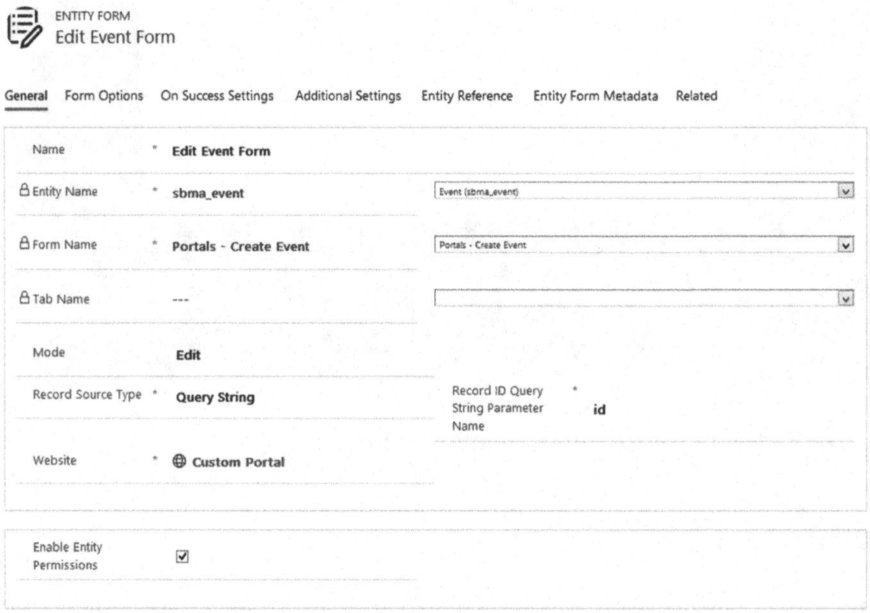

Figure 3-35.   *Edit form settings*

To enforce security, click the Enable Entity Permissions checkbox so that the users with event administration rights will be able to edit the event details. Next, open the entity list, navigate to the Options tab, click +Edit to add the edit button, and select the entity form created for editing the record (Figure 3-36).

112

Figure 3-36. *Adding edit form settings to the entity list*

In the portal, clicking the event code will open the edit form where users can edit the records and submit the changes (Figure 3-37).

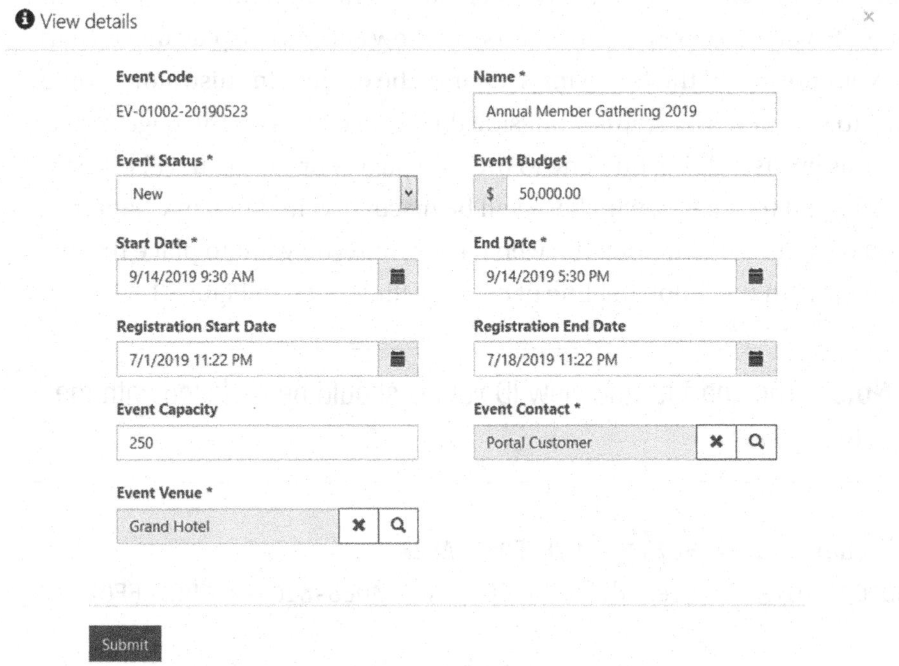

Figure 3-37. *Edit form*

What if the user does not have edit permissions for the record? When the user clicks the record to edit, the message shown in Figure 3-38 will be displayed.

113

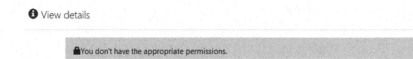

Figure 3-38. *Error message when the user does not have appropriate permissions*

Adding Charts to the Portal

Sometimes users want to see some graphical representation of data within the portal. Charts can be used to facilitate such requirements. In Dynamics 365 CE, you can easily create charts, but how can you display those charts in your portal? In the following scenario, the event administrators would like to see events by status alongside the list of events on the page. You can do this by just adding one line to the web page. For this, you will have to use Liquid templates, which we will be discussing in detail in Chapter 5 and Chapter 6. First, open the web page where you want to place the chart and paste in the following line of code, as illustrated in Figure 3-39.

Note   The chart ID and view ID values should be replaced with the actual values.

```
{% chart id:"F2B62346-F67E-E911-A828-
000D3AE01F57"  viewid:"A8A49CE1-C303-4DE8-8104-32FBC1FEF02F" %}
```

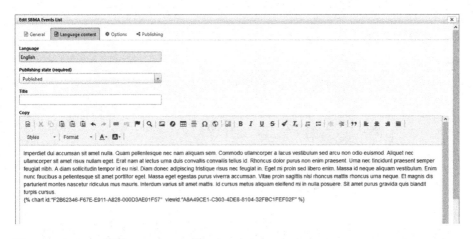

Figure 3-39. *Web content editor*

You can also add the Liquid line by opening the web page in the portals Dynamics 365 CE portal admin application and scrolling down to the inline grid where it lists the localized content (Figure 3-40).

Figure 3-40. *Localized content*

Open the entry, scroll down to the Content section, and enter the Liquid line, as shown in Figure 3-41.

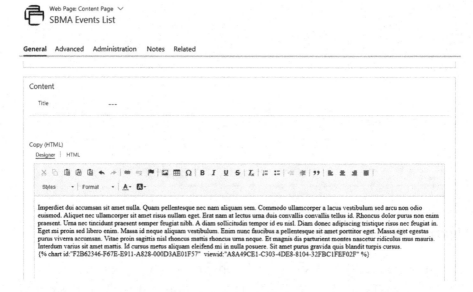

Figure 3-41. *Content editor, CRM portal app*

Save the settings and refresh the portal page to see the results
(Figure 3-42).

Figure 3-42. *Chart displayed on the web page*

You should always make sure the visiting user has the appropriate access rights; otherwise, the chart will not be visible to the users (Figure 3-43).

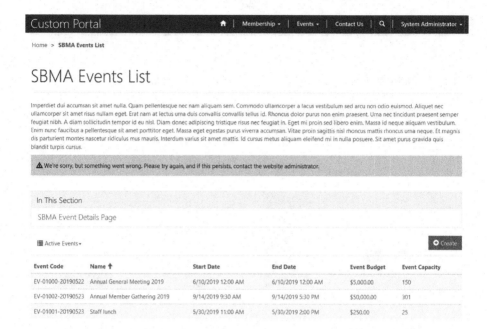

Figure 3-43. *The user does not have appropriate permission to view the chart*

Performing Validations

When capturing the data using forms, you must use proper validation techniques to ensure the integrity of the data. Incorrect data may result in unexpected behavior or erroneous outcomes in the business processes. In this section, you will look at some validation techniques that can be used with Dynamics 365 portals.

With Dynamics 365 CE configuration, you can enforce some validations, such as checking the length of a value entered in a field, setting fields as Business Required, and so on. For instance, when you set a field as Business Required in a Dynamics 365 CE form, the same validation will be rendered to the web form as well (Figure 3-44). As you can see in the figure, there are a few fields that are mandatory.

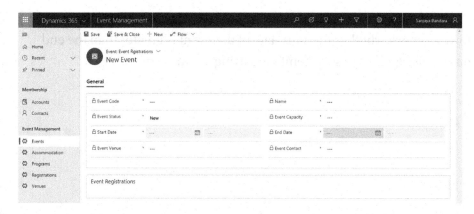

Figure 3-44. *Mandatory fields on the Dynamics 365 CE form*

Now, if this form is set up as an entity form in the portal, all the fields which are configured as mandatory in Dynamics 365 CE will also be mandatory on the entity form (as shown in Figure 3-45).

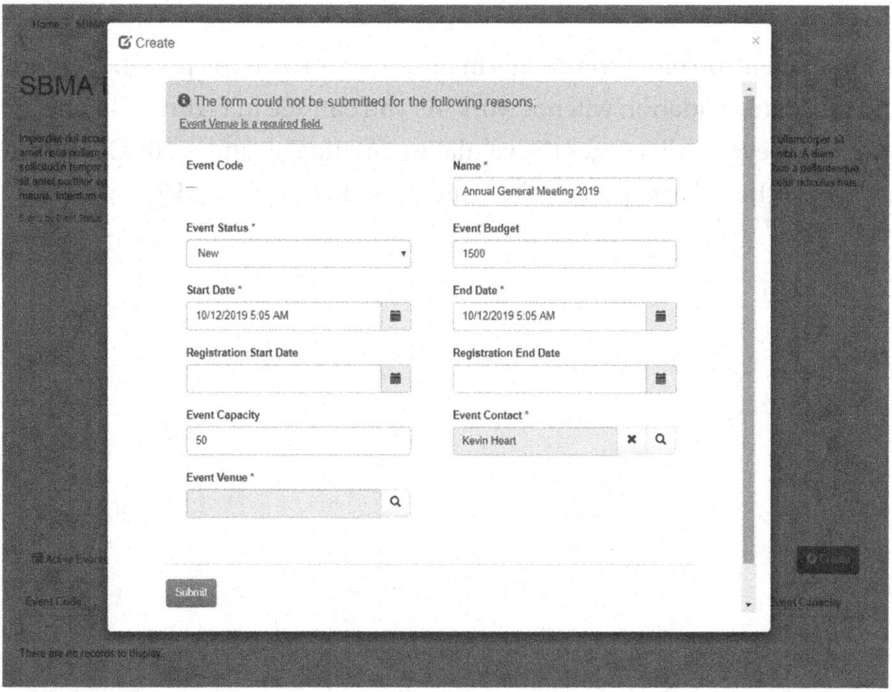

Figure 3-45. *Mandatory field validations*

As shown in Figure 3-46, there is a validation on the Dynamics 365 CE form to check whether the start date of the event is greater than the end date. This validation is implemented using business rules.

Figure 3-46. *Business rule validations on Dynamics 365 CE form*

But when you enter the details in the entity form in the portal, the start and end date validation will not work. As you can see in Figure 3-46, the on-change event will trigger the validation on the Dynamics 365 CE form. Let's enter the information via the entity form in the portal (Figure 3-47).

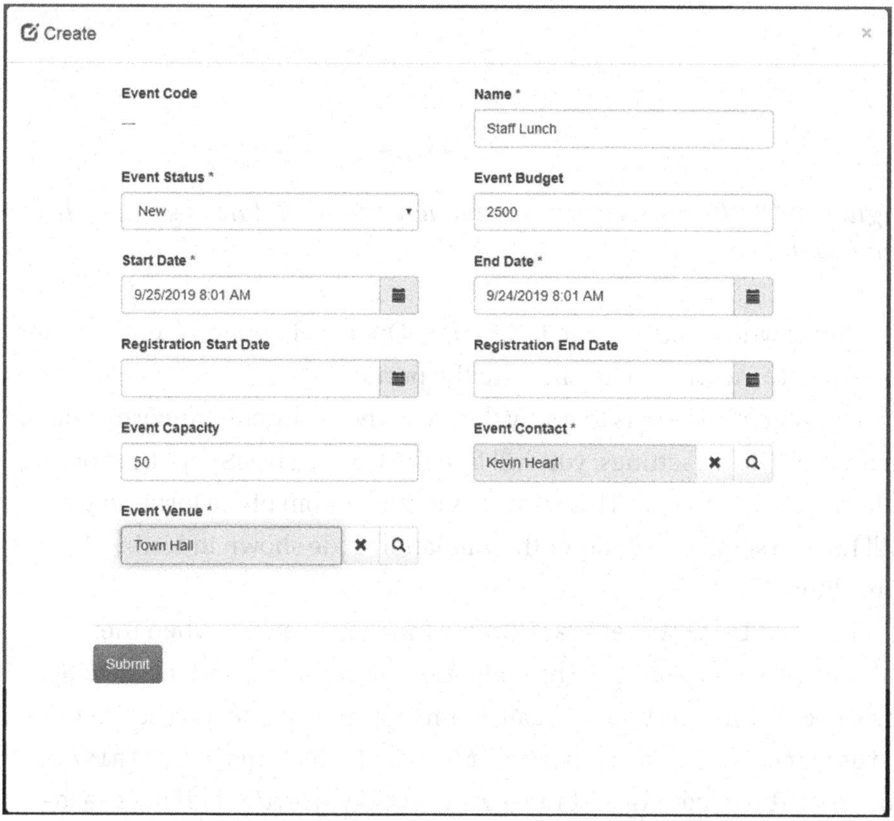

Figure 3-47. *Creating event records, with start and end date validations*

No validation gets triggered, and the record gets saved straightaway. At the time of writing this book, the business rules are not rendered in Dynamics 365 portals. As you can see in Figure 3-48, there are two records saved with incorrect start and end dates.

Event Code	Name ↑	Start Date	End Date	Ticket Price	Event Capacity
EV-01000-20190906	AGM 2019	10/1/2019 7:57 AM	9/30/2019 7:57 AM		50
EV-01001-20190906	Staff Lunch	9/25/2019 8:01 AM	9/24/2019 8:01 AM		50

Figure 3-48. *Event records saved where the start date is greater than the end date*

This is where you can use JavaScript/jQuery validation on entity forms to eliminate incorrect data entry via the portal.

Our objective here is to notify the user when they enter incorrect data. In the entity form settings, you will find the Custom JavaScript field on the Additional Settings tab. This section is at the bottom of the form, so you will have to scroll down. Enter the validation code shown in Listing 3-1 in the editor.

The entityFormClientValidation function executes when the submit button is executed. The code uses this function, and the specific logic goes inside this function call. For more information, please refer to https://community.adxstudio.com/products/adxstudio-portals/documentation/configuration-guide/entity-form/attributes-and-relationships/custom-javascript/.

Listing 3-1. Start and End Date Validation Code

```
if (window.jQuery) {
    (function ($) {
        if (typeof (entityFormClientValidate) != 'undefined') {
            var originalValidationFunction = entityFormClientValidate;
            if (originalValidationFunction && typeof
            (originalValidationFunction) == "function") {
                entityFormClientValidate = function() {
                    originalValidationFunction.apply(this, arguments);
                    var startDate = new Date($("#sbma_startdate").val());
```

```
        var endDate = new Date($("#sbma_enddate").val());
        if(startDate > endDate)
        {
            alert("Start date cannot be greater than end
            date.");
            return;
        }
    };
    }
  }
}(window.jQuery));
}
```

Now on the entity form, when you enter the wrong date range and hit Submit, the validation message will pop up (Figure 3-49).

Figure 3-49. *Incorrect date range validation message*

Until the user enters the correct value range, the validation will trigger.

Summary

This chapter explained how to modify the look and feel of a portal and how a portal can be configured to list and enter data. In this chapter, I covered applying themes, editing the content, adding entity lists, and creating entity forms. Also, I covered how entity forms can be associated with a list to enter and edit data. In the next chapter, we will be looking at another interesting customization known as web forms, and I will cover how to bind the portal with SharePoint for document management.

CHAPTER 4

Web Forms and Document Management

In this chapter, I'll discuss web forms and document management. Web forms are like entity forms, but there are some key features such as multistep navigation and branching logic that precede the entity forms. Especially when there are multiple steps involved in the data entry flow, then web forms are the ideal choice.

This chapter will dig deep into the various features and how they can be implemented to give the best experience to the user. As discussed in earlier chapters, Dynamics 365 for Customer Engagement supports SharePoint online integration, and now Dynamics 365 portals also support the ability to upload documents to SharePoint and display them on an entity or web form. This exposes the document management capabilities to the end users as well. Let's first look at web forms.

Web Forms

Web forms are a way to enter data through a portal to Dynamics 365 CE, especially in scenarios where there are multiple forms or a form has multiple tabs. Basically, a web form holds an association with web pages,

© Sanjaya Yapa 2019
S. Yapa, *Getting Started with Dynamics 365 Portals*,
https://doi.org/10.1007/978-1-4842-5346-5_4

and a start step is specified, which is used to control the initialization of the form within the portal. This association between the web form and the web page permits users to retrieve the form definition of a page within a web site. One might argue that using entity forms is much easier, but there are a few attractive features that can be used in certain situations. Table 4-1 lists some of the key differences and similarities between these two modes of data entry.

Table 4-1. *Comparison of Data Entry Modes: Web Forms vs. Entity Forms*

Web Forms	Entity Forms
Web forms utilize the same CrmEntityFormView control to render Dynamics 365 CE forms.	An entity or a managed form is a single form rendered by the CrmEntityFormView control.
Web forms do not require any developer intervention to add new forms.	Exposing this form requires a developer or power user to do the configuration.
One of the key features is that web forms support multiple-step forms.	A form does not support multiple pages or a wizard-like approach to capture the data.
Web forms support conditional branching between forms.	A form does not support conditional branching between forms.
Web forms have some additional properties that can be used to overcome the Dynamics 365 CE entity metadata and form designer limitations.	

In this example, we will be looking at the event registration scenario where a registrant/member logs in and registers for the desired event. Figure 4-1 illustrates the process flow.

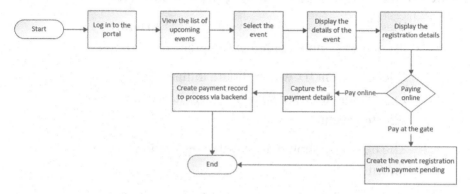

Figure 4-1. *Event registration flow*

Note   In this flow, the registrant can select to pay online or pay at the gate. In a situation where the registrant is paying online, then the credit card information must be captured. In this example, the information is captured and deleted when the payments are processed as a batch. You can also integrate a payment gateway, and you can find more information at https://docs.microsoft.com/en-au/dynamics365/customer-engagement/marketing/event-payment-gateway.

You can also find a full end-to-end event management scenario at https://docs.microsoft.com/en-au/dynamics365/customer-engagement/marketing/event-management.

Create a Web Form

First, we need to identify the steps involved in the process by looking at Figure 4-1. As you can see, the following steps are involved:

1. View the list of upcoming events. This is an entity list that was implemented in Chapter 3 of this book.

2. Click the event ID, which should initiate the registration flow by displaying the details of the selected event.

3. The next page should display the registration information.

4. On this page, the registrant can elect to pay online or pay at the gate.

5. Complete the registration.

To create the web form, click the Web Forms option in the Content menu of the left pane and click +New, as shown in Figure 4-2.

Figure 4-2. *Creating a new web form*

On the new web form, there are a few settings that you should set, as shown in Figure 4-3. As you can see, the Name and Website settings are mandatory. You can set the starting step once all the web form steps have been defined. This will be the step where the process will start. Even if there is only one step, it will be the starting step. That is, you can have web forms where only one step is used.

You can also see that Start New Session On Load is set to Yes. When this is set to No, when a user starts a session for registering, all the data in the steps will be cached if they leave and come back later. There is a good side and a bad side to this. Sometimes a registrant might want to start the registration at the point where they stopped or accidentally closed the browser window. You should set this option to No if you have complex forms with lots of data to fill in.

The Multiple Records Per User setting will always depend on the business requirements. If the user is allowed to create multiple records, then this setting should be set to Yes, as shown in Figure 4-3.

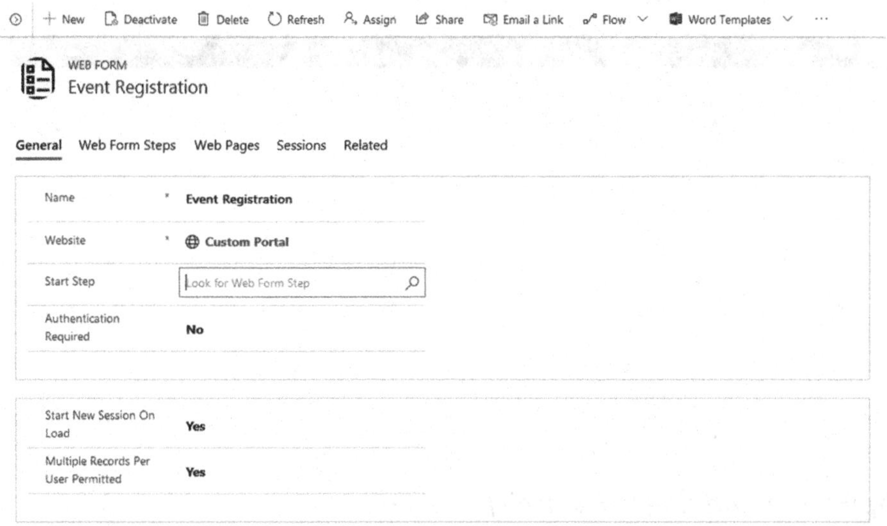

Figure 4-3. New web form settings

Once the form is saved, the next step is to add the web form steps to the web form.

Web Form Steps

Web form steps are used to define the flow logic of the web form. These web form steps can also be configured for conditional branching and to redirect users to where the process initiated or to a different location. In a scenario where you have configured multiple steps, you need to remember that every web form step will contain a pointer to the next step. But terminal steps will not have a pointer. To learn more, please refer to https://docs.microsoft.com/en-us/dynamics365/customer-engagement/portals/web-form-steps.

You will define the web form steps on the Web Form Steps tab, as shown in Figure 4-4. The grid on this screen lists all the web form steps that you add to the web form. To add a new step, click the +Add New Web Form Step button on the grid toolbar.

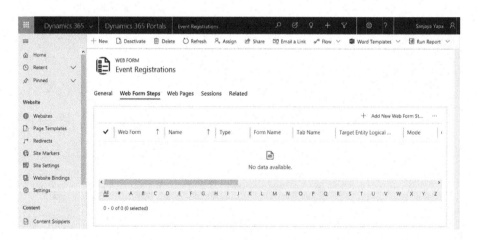

Figure 4-4. *Adding a new web form step*

As per the requirements, the first step should display the event details when you click the event link in the upcoming events lists. See Figure 4-5.

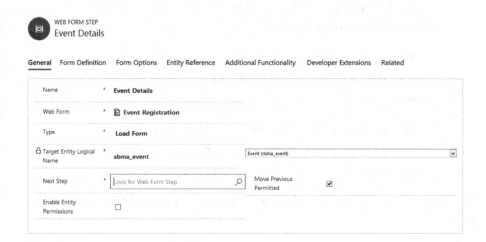

Figure 4-5. *Web form step settings*

The following settings must be specified on the General tab of the Web Form Step form:

- **Name**: This is the name of the web form and is a required field.

- **Web Form**: This is the parent web form that this step belongs to.

- **Type**: This can be one of the following types:

  - Load Form/Tab, which displays the properties of a form or a tab

  - Redirect, which defines step properties to redirect to a specific URL/page

  - Condition, which defines the expressions to be evaluated for branching the steps based on a condition

131

- **Target entity logical name**: This is the logical name of the target entity associated with this step.

- **Next Step**: This property defines the next step, which the flow should move to.

- **Move Previous Permitted**: When this property is checked, the user can navigate back to the previous step.

- **Enable Entity Permissions**: If you want to enforce entity permissions on the web form step, then select this option.

On the Form Definition tab, you must specify the settings as shown in Figure 4-6.

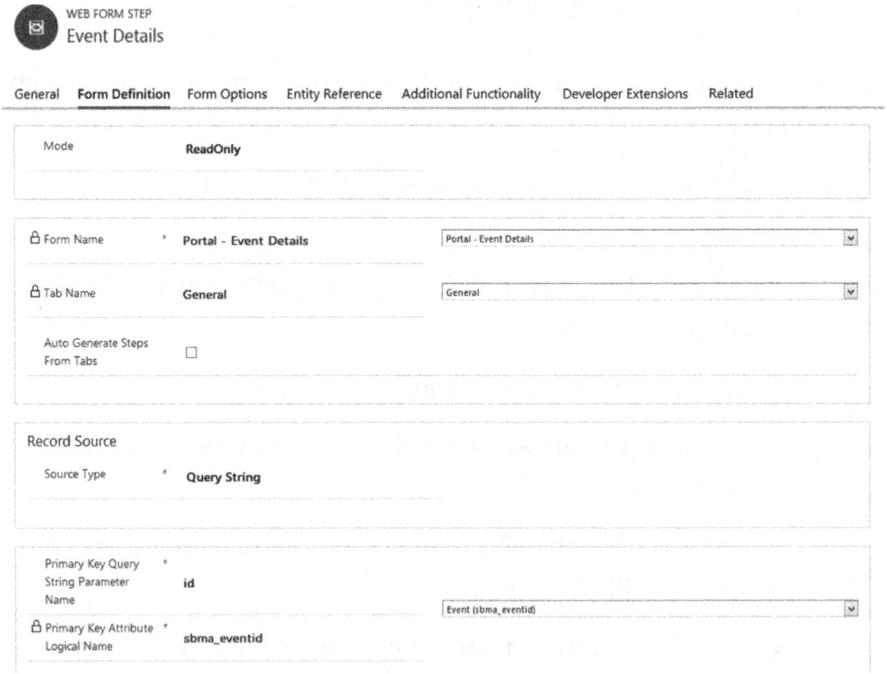

Figure 4-6. *Web form step: form definition settings*

As mentioned earlier, in this step we will be displaying the details of the form for the registrant to see. Therefore, you should make the settings read-only.

- **Mode:** When this option is set to Read Only, the form fields will be uneditable.

- **Form Name:** This is the name of the Dynamics 365 CE form to be used. You can also define specific forms in Dynamics 365 CE only for web forms, just to display the required information only.

- **Tab Name:** If there are multiple tabs and your intention is to display only one specific tab, then select the tab from the drop-down.

- **Auto Generate Steps from Tabs:** You can also automatically generate the steps for the tabs.

- **Record Source:** This is where to get the record sources for this step.

- **Source Type:** We will be using Query String, which means the ID for the record will be passed via the query string parameter.

- **Primary Key Query String Parameter Name:** This is the name of the parameter that you will be using.

- **Primary Key Attribute Logical Name:** This is the attribute name of the parameter that is passed.

For the first step, these settings are enough. There are other settings that will be explained for the other steps. Now you can specify the start step for the parent web form (Figure 4-7).

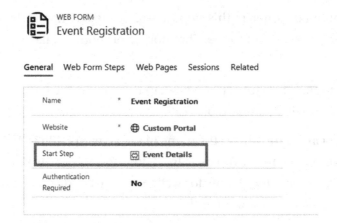

Figure 4-7. *Setting the start step*

When the registrant selects the event and clicks the event code, the process will be initiated and will display the details of the event, as shown in Figure 4-8.

Figure 4-8. *Web form step 1, loading event details*

The next step is to define the Event Registration Details step. The settings on the General tab are the same as defined for the previous step. Figure 4-9 illustrates them.

Important   The next step of the Event Registration Flow can be defined with the next form step "Event Registration Details" which capture the registrant information. Then it will be the next step of the current step which is the Event Details step.

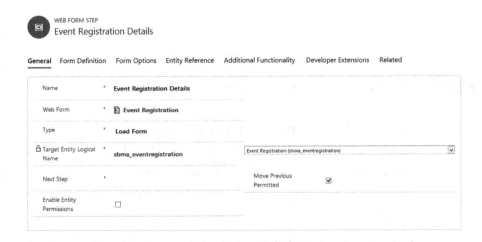

Figure 4-9.   *Event Registration Details step*

On the Form Definition tab, you need to set the following settings. Since this step is for creating a new event registration, the settings are slightly different than before, as shown in Figure 4-10.

WEB FORM STEP
Event Registration Details

General **Form Definition** Form Options Entity Reference Additional Functionality Developer Extensions Related

Mode	Insert

🔒 Form Name	* Main Information	Main Information ⌄
🔒 Tab Name	General	General ⌄
Auto Generate Steps From Tabs	☑	

Record Source	
Source Type	---

Figure 4-10. Event registration details, form definition

- **Mode**: This is set to Insert because we are going to create a new record. You must remember that when a step is set to Insert mode, as soon as the user hits the Next/Submit button in this step, the record will be created.

  You can see that the Source Type setting under Record Source is blank. This is basically because we are creating a new record and not necessarily relying on information passed from previous steps. But we need the details of the event to set the reference on the event registration form. Ideally, the form lookup for Event should be automatically filled in when loading the form step. To set these up, open the Entity Reference tab of the web form step and set the properties as shown in Figure 4-11.

Figure 4-11. *Setting entity references for the form*

- **Set Entity Reference on Save**: When this property is toggled to Yes, the rest of the properties will appear to set the entity reference when saving the record.

- **Entity Logical Name**: This is the logical name of the parent entity of the relationship.

- **Relationship Name**: This is the name given to the relationship.

- **Target Lookup Attribute Logical Name**: This is the lookup attribute of the relationships.

- **Entity Reference Source**: This defines how you would get the reference for the field.

- **Source Type**: The source type is set to the query string to pass the data as the query string.

- **Query String Name**: This is the name of the query string parameter.

- **Query String Attribute Logical Name**: This is the logical name of the attribute passed with the query string.

Once these settings are defined, you can save and move on to define the properties of the next step. Always remember to set the Next Step property of the previous step once the current step is completed.

The web form, is similar to the form illustrated in Figure 4-12. You can see the entity references are set automatically per the configuration.

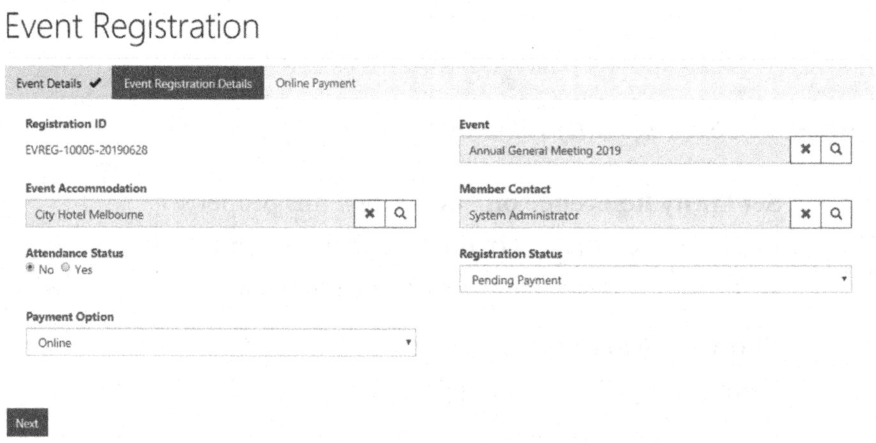

Event Registration

Figure 4-12. *The event registration step*

Conditional Branching

Conditional branching is for directing the flow of the process based on a given condition. In this example, we are going to capture payment information if the registrant elects to pay online. If the registrant elects to pay at the gate, then the registration is created, and the user is directed back to the event list. For this purpose, you should create a web form step of type Condition, as shown in Figure 4-13.

Figure 4-13. *Conditional web form step*

On the General tab when you select the Target Entity Logical Name setting, it should be the logical name of the entity to which the condition will be applicable. For this example, we will be applying the condition to the Payment Type field of the Event Registration entity. To define the condition, navigate to the Condition tab. As you can see in Figure 4-14, configuring the condition is easy. Even the help text on the form itself gives you a starting point to define the condition. For more information, you can visit https://docs.microsoft.com/en-us/dynamics365/customer-engagement/portals/add-conditional-step.

Figure 4-14. *Defining the condition for the Condition web form step*

You should also remember to specify the property Next Step if Condition Fails, which defines where the flow should go if the condition fails. For this example, we have specified the redirect step to direct the flow back to the page where the process was initiated.

Redirect Step

By default, when the flow logic completes, a success message is displayed, and the user must navigate back to where the process was started or to a specific location in the portal. While this approach is acceptable to some degree, when considering the user experience, it is not the best practice. Ideally, when the registration process completes, the user should be automatically directed to a specific location. This is where the redirect step is valuable. For this example, configure the settings as shown in Figure 4-15.

As you can see, the settings on the General tab are not much different from the other steps. The most important property that you should always set is Target Entity Logical Name. In this example, it is set to the Events entity since the flow should redirect back to the Events entity list. Keep the Next Step property blank.

WEB FORM STEP
Redirect to Events

General   Redirect   Developer Extensions   Related

Name	*	**Redirect to Events**
Web Form	*	📄 **Event Registration**
Type	*	**Redirect**
🔒 Target Entity Logical Name		**sbma_event** Event (sbma_event) ▾
Next Step	*	--- Move Previous Permitted ☑
Enable Entity Permissions		☐

Figure 4-15. *Setting up the redirect step*

The next step is to define where to redirect the flow, which you must do on the Redirect tab of the step, as shown in Figure 4-16. You have two options to direct the flow. In a scenario where you want to direct the flow to another URL, specify the URL in the External URL box, or if you want to direct the flow to a web page within a Dynamics 365 portal, then select the specific web page from the lookup. As mentioned earlier, for this example we will be using the Web Page option.

WEB FORM STEP
Redirect to Events

General   **Redirect**   Developer Extensions   Related

External URL	---		
or Web Page	🗐 SBMA Event List for Registrations		
Append Existing Query String	**No**		
Append Entity ID To Query String	☐	Query String Name	---
Append Custom Query String	---		

Append an attribute's value to the Query String

Query String Parameter Name	---
🔒 Attribute Logical Name	---

Figure 4-16. *Setting the redirect location*

Those are the basics of web forms in Dynamics 365 portals. In the next section, I cover some custom code used with portals.

Custom Code

In Dynamics 365 portals, you can use jQuery to extend the capabilities of the platform. The following are a few examples of how you can use jQuery. In the following example, when the user clicks an event, it will display the event details. On the event details page, there is a register button to start the registration process.

1. Add the custom HTML Button by opening the web page where you want to add the custom button and adding the HTML code to the Content section of the web form, as shown in Figure 4-17.

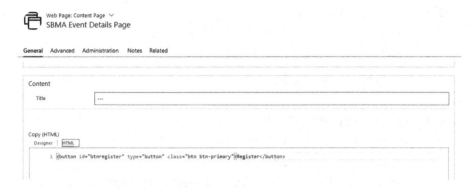

Figure 4-17. *HTML custom button*

Make sure you give a proper ID to the button because you need to use a jQuery selector to access the button.

2. Now that we have added the button, we need to trigger the process. On the Advanced tab, you will find the editor to enter the JavaScript, as shown in Figure 4-18.

Figure 4-18. *JavaScript editor*

```
$.urlParam = function(name){
    var results = new RegExp('[/\?&]' + name +
    '=([^&#]*)').exec(window.location.href);
    return results[1] || 0;
}
$(document).ready(function(){
    $("#btnregister").click(function(){
        var eventId = $.urlParam('id');
        window.location.href = '/upcomingevents/EventRegistration/
        ?id='+eventId;
    });
});
```

This code will read the url parameter and pass it into the next step, which is the registration process. Instead of relying on the out-of-the-box web forms, you can create your own registration process with integrated payments. To learn more about custom code, please refer to https:// docs.microsoft.com/en-us/dynamics365/customer-engagement/ portals/add-custom-javascript.

SharePoint Integration

Dynamics 365 portals support integration with SharePoint to manage documents. There are scenarios where the portal users must submit additional documents as evidence, such as in a member registration scenario or even a scanned copy of the member registration. As we all know, Microsoft SharePoint is a widely used document management solution , and it integrates with Dynamics 365 CE seamlessly. The portals now support uploading and displaying documents from within an entity form or a web form in a portal. This extends the portal's user capabilities by allowing them to directly upload documents to the SharePoint document library.

Important   The document management features work only with SharePoint online and are supported with server-based integration.

To enable the document management capabilities of the Dynamics portals, you must perform the following actions:

1. Enable document management in Dynamic 365 CE.

2. Enable document management for the required entities.

3. Enable SharePoint integration from the portal Admin Center.

4. Configure the Dynamics CE forms to list the documents.

5. Create the required entity permissions and assign the required web role.

Let's look at each step one at a time.

Enable Document Management in Dynamics 365 CE

First, you must enable the server-based document management functionality for Dynamics 365 CE. By default, your Dynamics 365 CE users are not allowed to access your SharePoint sites. You must provide the required access levels from SharePoint. You must be an Office 365 Global Administrator to perform this action.

Note   The images used in this section were captured in the new Admin Center.

1. Navigate to the Microsoft 365 Admin Center and launch SharePoint. This action will take you to the SharePoint Admin Center (Figure 4-19).

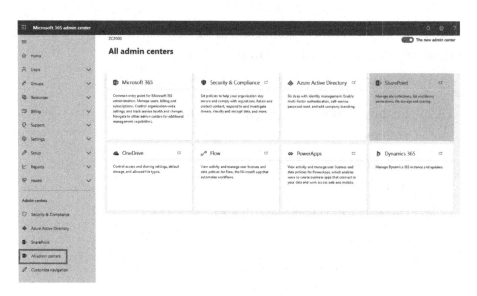

Figure 4-19. *Microsoft 365 Admin Center*

2. You must share the SharePoint site so that portal users can access it. This all depends on what level of access your client wants their users to have. You can find more about external sharing at `https://sharegate.com/blog/ultimate-guide-deal-with-office-365-external-sharing#what-is-sharing`. See Figure 4-20.

Figure 4-20. *Sharing the SharePoint site to portal users*

3. Now you should enable the document management in Dynamics 365 CE. Under Settings, click Document Management. On this page, you will find the option Enable Server-Based SharePoint Integration. See Figure 4-21.

Figure 4-21. *SharePoint server integration*

The setup process is a simple wizard that takes you through the configuration. As shown in Figure 4-22, you must make sure the Online option is selected.

Figure 4-22. *Enabling server-based SharePoint integration, step 1*

On the next page, you must specify the URL of the site. As shown in Figure 4-23, enter the site URL and click Next.

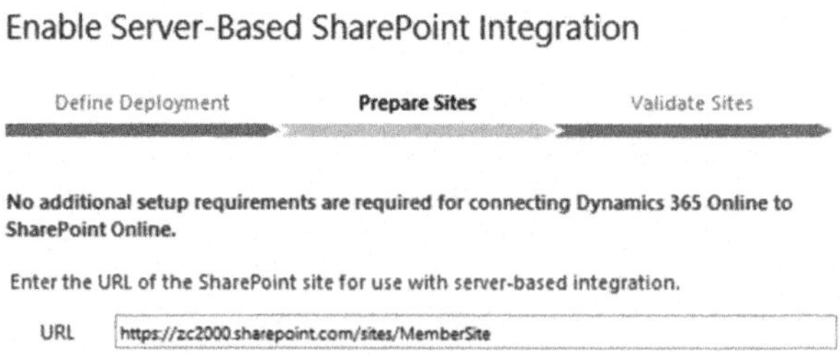

Enable Server-Based SharePoint Integration

Define Deployment	**Prepare Sites**	Validate Sites

No additional setup requirements are required for connecting Dynamics 365 Online to SharePoint Online.

Enter the URL of the SharePoint site for use with server-based integration.

URL	https://zc2000.sharepoint.com/sites/MemberSite

Figure 4-23. *Entering a SharePoint site URL*

When the Next button is clicked, you can see the process validate the URL, and if everything is in place, a Validation Succeeded message will be displayed. Click the Finish button.

Enable Document Management for the Required Entities

Now, in Document Management Settings, select the entities for which you want to enable the document management function, as shown in Figure 4-24.

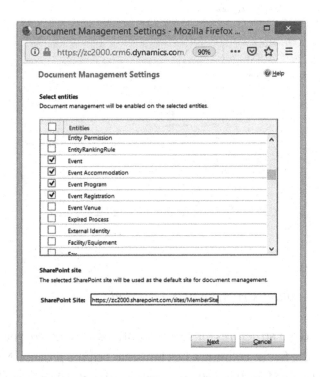

Figure 4-24. *Selecting the entities for which to enable document management*

The Document Management Setting is available in the Document Management section of the Settings area of Dynamics 365 CE. When you select this option, you will be asked to select the folder structure. If folder structure is account-based, then select the folder structure given, and the folders will be created accordingly. For this demo, we will not be selecting this option. You can see the folder structure being created (see Figure 4-25).

Figure 4-25. *Folder structure being created*

Once the folder structures for selected entities are created, you will see Succeeded in the Status column. Click Finish to exit the process. Now, when you navigate to the SharePoint site, you will see that the document libraries for the selected entities have been created, as shown in Figure 4-26.

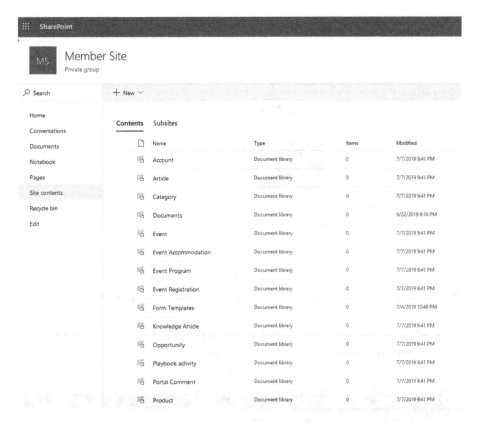

Figure 4-26. *Document libraries created in the SharePoint site*

Enable SharePoint Integration from the Portal Admin Center

The next step is to enable the SharePoint integration in the portal so that the document libraries hosted in SharePoint can be accessed from the portal. Navigate to the portal Admin Center and select "Set up SharePoint integration." You can see the option "Enable SharePoint integration," as shown in Figure 4-27.

Figure 4-27. *Enabling SharePoint integration for a portal*

When you click the toggle button, it will prompt you with the message shown in Figure 4-28. Click the Enable button.

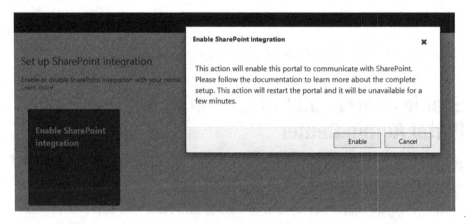

Figure 4-28. *Confirming SharePoint integration for a portal*

This process will take a few minutes, and the site will be unavailable during this time. Also, you will be prompted with the message illustrated in Figure 4-29. Click Accept.

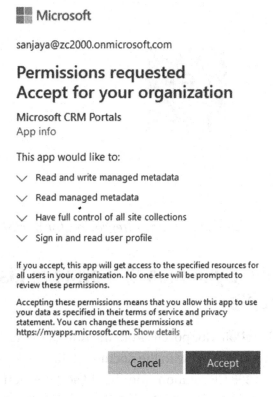

Figure 4-29. Accepting permission requirements

Important   If you are performing this action for a production site, then appropriate communication should be done before this step to inform the portal user. That is, if this feature is enabled on an existing site, then the portal users must be informed because the portal will be unavailable for a few minutes.

When the integration is successfully enabled, then the toggle button will change to "Disable SharePoint integration," as shown in Figure 4-30.

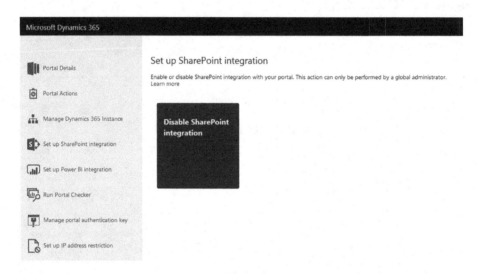

Figure 4-30. *Enabling SharePoint integration for portals*

Configure the Dynamics CE Forms to List the Documents

After enabling SharePoint for portals from the Admin Center, you must configure the form to interact with the document library. This is done through Dynamics 365 CE solution. You should add the required subgrid to list the documents to the form. Make sure you select Document Location for the Entity property, and the Default view should be Active Document Locations, as shown in Figure 4-31.

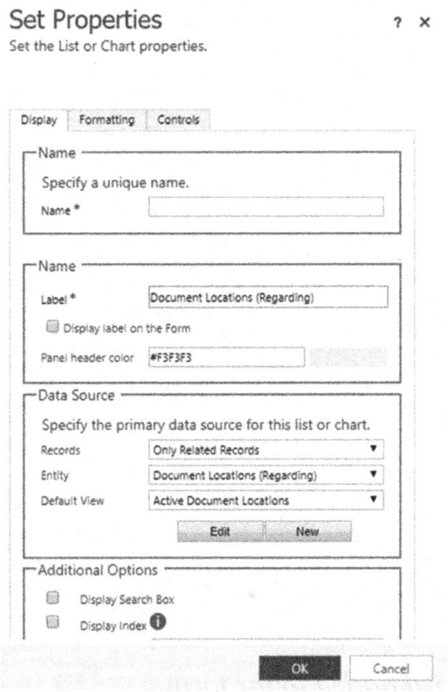

Figure 4-31. *Setting the subgrid properties*

Once you add the subgrid to the form, your form should look like
Figure 4-32.

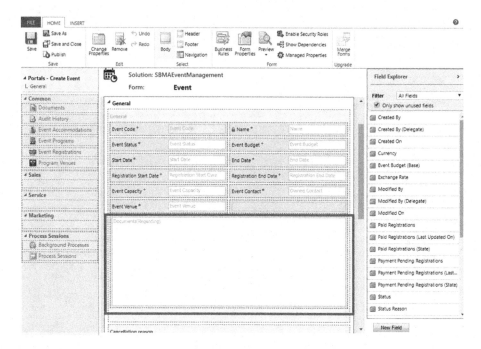

Figure 4-32. *Subgrid added to the form*

Create the Required Entity Permissions

Now that you have updated the interface, the next step is to create the entity permissions so that users with the appropriate permissions will have access to the document management functions available through the SharePoint integration. Since the SharePoint locations are mapped to Dynamics 365 CE via the Document Location entity, you must provide entity permissions to the Document Location entity, as shown in Figure 4-33.

Figure 4-33. *Document Location entity permissions*

Then append the entity permission to the web role. In this example, it is the Event Admin web role (Figure 4-34).

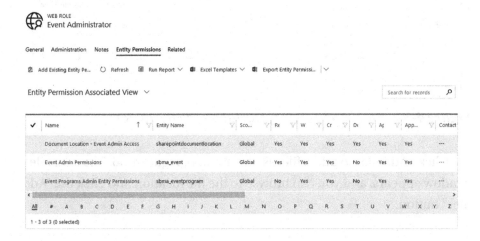

Figure 4-34. *Appending the entity permissions to the web role*

Now that all the steps for configuring the SharePoint integration are completed, let's test this. As you can see in Figure 4-35, at the bottom of the Event Details page you can see the document subgrid.

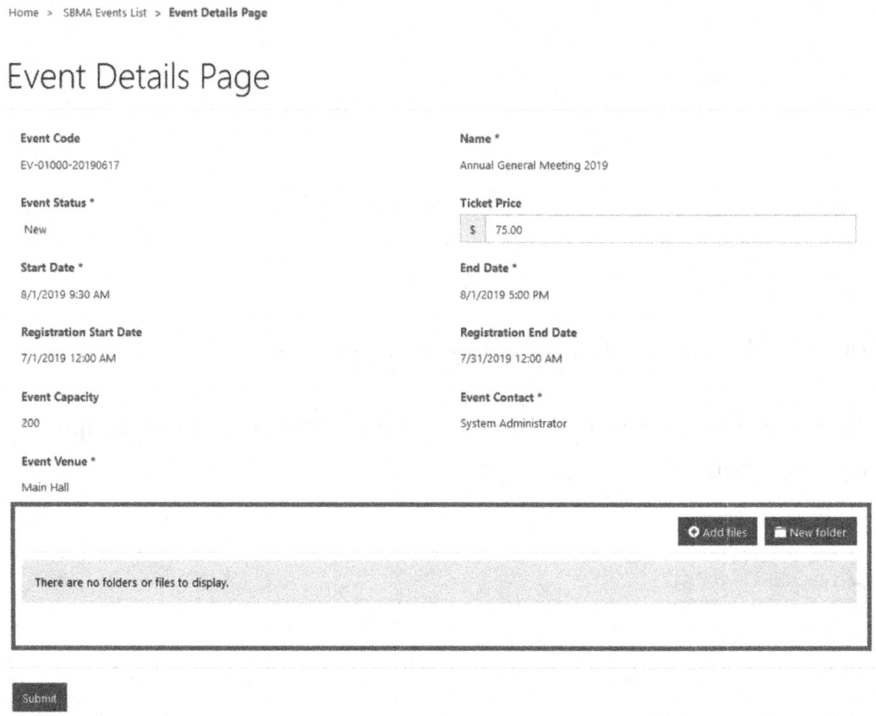

Home > SBMA Events List > **Event Details Page**

Event Details Page

Event Code	**Name** *
EV-01000-20190617	Annual General Meeting 2019
Event Status *	**Ticket Price**
New	$ 75.00
Start Date *	**End Date** *
8/1/2019 9:30 AM	8/1/2019 5:00 PM
Registration Start Date	**Registration End Date**
7/1/2019 12:00 AM	7/31/2019 12:00 AM
Event Capacity	**Event Contact** *
200	System Administrator
Event Venue *	
Main Hall	

⊕ Add files   🖿 New folder

There are no folders or files to display.

Submit

Figure 4-35. *Document library portal on the portal form*

Click +Add files to add a file, as illustrated in Figure 4-36. The Add Files window appears, and you can browse to the file location and click the "Add files" button.

Add files   ×

Choose files   Browse...   SampleFileWord.docx

                        ☑ Overwrite existing files

                                              Add files   Cancel

Figure 4-36. *"Add files" pop-up window*

And now, on the web form, you will be able to see the files attached to the record, as shown in Figure 4-37.

Name ↑	Modified	
📄 SampleFileWord.docx (19 KB)	less than a minute ago	⌄
📄 SampleFileWord.pdf (24 KB)	less than a minute ago	⌄

Submit

Figure 4-37. *Files attached to the record on the web form*

In Dynamics 365 CE, when you open the event record, you will see the files you have uploaded. See Figure 4-38.

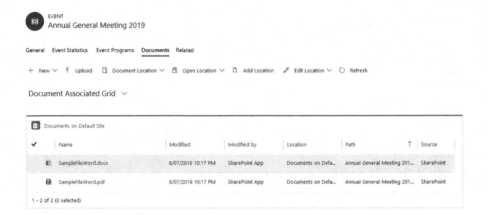

Figure 4-38. *Files uploaded in Dynamics 365 CE*

Also, when you open the SharePoint document library and navigate to the folder dedicated to the event record, you will see the same files, as shown in Figure 4-39. Remember, the SharePoint document library is the ultimate destination for the documents you uploaded. Dynamics 365 CE and the portal are just a view into this folder.

Note   This integration is the default integration, but there could be specific integration requirements such as the client might have a unique folder structure. In such scenarios, you might have to come up with additional designs and code implementations.

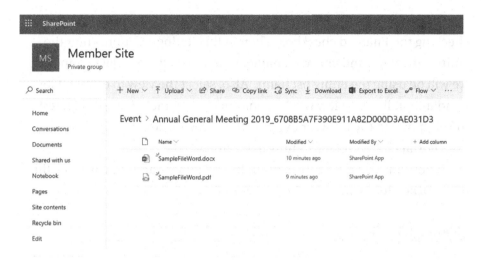

Figure 4-39. *Files in the SharePoint document library*

OData and Custom Forms

In this section, we will be using the OData feed in a Dynamics 365 portal to retrieve and submit data. This capability of Dynamics 365 portals is useful in scenarios where complex logic needs to be implemented. Let's first create an entity list and associate it with a web page. Once the entity list is created, navigate to the OData tab of the entity list form (Figure 4-40).

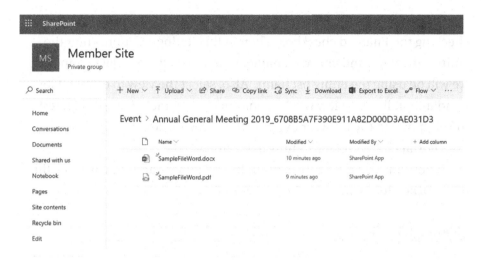

Figure 4-40. *OData feed settings of entity list*

On this screen, the first thing you must do is enable the OData feed by checking the Enabled checkbox. Then in the Settings section, enter the entity type name and entity set name. When we call the OData endpoint, we will be using the entity list name. Also, select the view to extract data. Fundamentally, this view will be your query to extract data. You can test the endpoint in the browser by using the following format:

<Portal URL>/_odata/<Entity Set Name>

When you enter the URL without the entity set name, you will see the list of OData feeds available in your portal (Figure 4-41).

Figure 4-41.   *OData feed list*

When you enter the URL with the entity list name, you can retrieve the data, as shown in Figure 4-42. As you can see, the result set is JSON. Now let's use this OData feed and create a new custom page that lists this data.

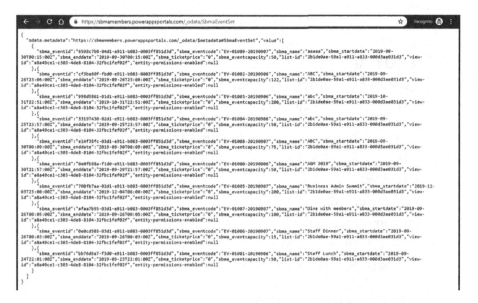

Figure 4-42. *OData result set*

Now let's create a new web page and open the entry in the Localized
Content area. Scroll down and enter the following code on the HTML tab:

```
<div style="text-align:right; width:100%; padding:0;">
<a href="#" class="btn btn-info">Create New event</a>
</div>
<div class="row" id="list" style="margin: 0px">
  <ul class="thumbnails" id="events">
     <li> </li>
  </ul>
</div>

<div class="overley" id="loading">
   <div class="content">
      <div>Loading...</div>
   </div>
```

```
<p>
  <script>
  //<![CDATA[
   $(document).ready(function(){
     $("#events").empty();

     var odataurl = "https://sbmamembers.powerappsportals.
     com/_odata/SbmaEventSet";
     $.ajax({
        type: "GET",
        url: odataurl,
        datatype: 'json'
     }).done(function(json){

     var eventsJson = json.value;

     $.each(eventsJson, function(index, sbmaevent){
$("#events").append("<div class='float-left panel panel-info'>
<div class='panel-heading'><h3 class='panel-title'>"+sbmaevent.
sbma_name+"</h3></div><div class='panel-body'><a id='evtdetails'
href='#'class='btn btn-primary'>"+sbmaevent.sbma_eventcode+
"</a><br><b>Start Date: </b>"+$.date(sbmaevent.sbma_startdate)
+"<br><b>End Date: </b>"+$.date(sbmaevent.sbma_enddate)
+"</div></div>")
        })
      $("#evtdetails").click(function(){
         alert("Loading event details");});
    }).always(function() {
    $("#loading").fadeOut();
  })
 });
```

```
$.date=(function(dateobject){
var d = new Date(dateobject);
  var day = d.getDate();
  var month = d.getMonth() + 1;
  var year = d.getFullYear();

  if (day < 10) {
     day = "0" + day;
  }
  if (month < 10) {
     month = "0" + month;
  }
  var date = day + "/" + month + "/" + year;
   return date;
  });

//]]>
    </script>
 </p>
</div>
```

This simple code demonstrates how you can use the OData feed. Here the OData feed is used to retrieve the data. The OData URL is passed to the Ajax request and retrieves data. When you open the web page, you will see the results, as shown in Figure 4-43.

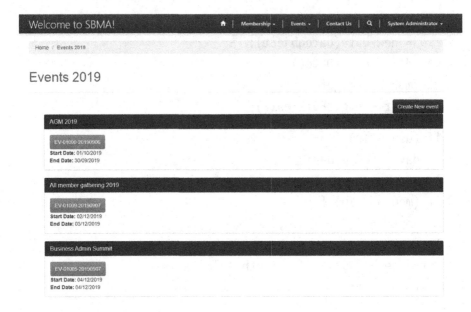

Figure 4-43. *Custom event list*

Important   At the time of writing this book, the OData feed is read-only. It does not support Create, Update, or Delete records. You could create an ASMX web service and deploy it to an Azure portal. This web service contains all the Create, Update, and Delete operations, and you can call these web methods and pass the parameters via the portal JavaScript. This is recommended only if the native features are not capable of implementing complex requirements.

Summary

In this chapter, you learned about web forms, custom coding, and SharePoint integration. These are some of the key out-of-the-box features. In the next chapter, I will be laying the foundation for advanced customizations of portals.

CHAPTER 5

Introduction to Liquid Templates

So far in this book I have discussed the out-of-the-box features of Dynamics 365 portals. These features are powerful, and you do not have to write a single line of code when using them. But there are scenarios where your clients or end users would like to make the portal's look and feel more attractive and user-friendly to their portal audience. As you have seen in the previous chapters, the default look and feel is a basic Bootstrap template. In addition, sometimes you might want to present data based on some given logic that the out-of-the-box features do not support. But with Liquid templates, you can overcome these limitations and make the portal more appealing to end users. In this chapter, you will be learning about the basics of Liquid templates. This will give you an understanding of the capabilities of the language.

What Is Liquid?

Liquid is a template engine that was originally developed by Shopify for internal purposes. But later Shopify made it open source. Initially it was written using the Ruby language, but later it was migrated to another open source project called DotLiquid. At the time of Adx Studio, before Liquid templates were used, it was hard to make minor changes to a portal because doing so would require a full deployment. But once Adx

© Sanjaya Yapa 2019
S. Yapa, *Getting Started with Dynamics 365 Portals*,
https://doi.org/10.1007/978-1-4842-5346-5_5

Studio incorporated Liquid templates, web content presentation and maintenance became much easier and robust. If you are interested in learning more about Liquid, refer to the Liquid documentation from Shopify at `https://help.shopify.com/en/themes/liquid`.

Keep in mind that Liquid templates can remove the complications and limitations of data presentation, even though you still have to configure and customize the Liquid templates in Dynamics 365 portals. For additional reading, there are other template languages, such as Handlebars (`http://handlebarsjs.com/`) and Moustache (`https://mustache.github.io/`), which have a similar syntax. You can find more information about Handlebars at `https://github.com/wycats/handlebars.js`. In the ASP.NET ecosystem, Razor provides a similar feature for embedding server-based code into web pages. But, for Dynamics 365 portals, Liquid is the template engine used.

Liquid templates consist of three main components.

- **Tags**: Tags define the programming logic of the template. Basically, they tell the template how to present data in a logical manner. Tags are written between the {% %} characters. There are a few different kinds of tags available: control flow tags, iteration tags, variable tags, template tags, and entity tags.

- **Filters**: Filters can be considered as simple functions/ methods that are used to modify the output of variables and objects. There are array filters, date filters, entity list filters, math filters, string filters, type filters, URL filters, and a few additional filters that define some general functionality.

- **Objects**: Objects are used to output dynamic content to a page. For instance, the page object has an attribute called title. You can use this to output the title of the current page. To access the object attribute, use a dot, and to render an object's attribute in a template, use the {{ }} characters. You can also use the string name and [ ] to access the attribute of an object. This is useful in scenarios where the title should be determined dynamically or when the attribute contains characters, spaces, etc., which could be invalid when using the dot syntax.

We will be looking at these components in details in the subsequent sections of this chapter. Liquid templates can be used in web pages, content snippets, and web templates.

Using Web Templates to Store the Source

A *web template* is a Dynamics 365 portal admin app record that is used to store the template content. Generally, a template contains the Liquid code to render the dynamic content. Web templates can be combined with other templates or included in other content by using the Name attribute of a tag. You can also create full-page templates or create custom headers and footers to extend the look and feel of your web portal. A web template consists of the following attributes:

- **Name:** This is the name of the template that is used to reference other content or templates.

- **Source**: This attribute contains the source code or the content of the web template. Out of the box, this field comes with a source code editor with syntax highlighting.

- **MIME type:** This attribute is used only when this template is associated with a page template, which controls the rendering of all content of that template. This attribute is an optional field, and if not provided, the default value will be text/HTML.

Using Web Templates

Web templates can be used with page templates and to override the global headers and footer.

As Page Templates

You can create a new page template using a web template without writing a single line of .NET code. The best part is you don't have to redeploy the application. To achieve this, when creating a new page template, make sure you set Type to Web Template, as shown in Figure 5-1.

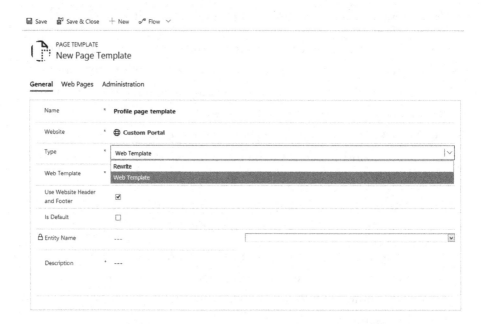

Figure 5-1. *Creating a new page template with Type set to Web Template*

As you can see, the option Use Website Header and Footer is selected by default, which means your web template will control the rendering of all page content between the global header and footer. If you uncheck this option, then your web template must render the entire response. If your template is rendering HTML, then this should include all the content from the doctype to the root HTML.

Web templates are commonly used to render HTML, but rendering an entire HTML response by unselecting the Use Website Header and Footer option will allow you to choose any text-based rendering format you desire. This is where MIME type rendering is handy. That is, when a page template is not using the header and footer rendering, the content type of the HTTP response header is set to the MIME type defined in the web template. The default value is text/HTML. For instance, you can set the MIME type to application/rss+xml to render an RSS feed.

To Replace Headers and Footers

You can use web templates to change the default header and footer of the web site. This can be done by simply changing the Header Template and Footer Template fields of the web site, as illustrated in Figure 5-2.

Important   Before making any changes, it is always a good idea to make a copy of the out of the box header and footer and use them as the starting point.

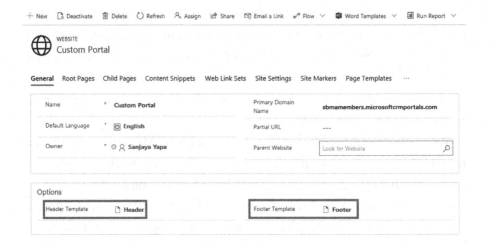

Figure 5-2. *Header and template fields of the web site*

Important   When you change the header template to a web template that you have created, then your template should take over the responsibility of rendering the primary navigation, sign-in/sign-out links, search interface, etc. Normally these functionalities are handled by the default header template.

When you navigate to the web templates section, you will find a whole list of default templates used within the default implementation. Visit this page for more information about these templates: https:// docs.microsoft.com/en-us/dynamics365/customer-engagement/ portals/store-content-web-templates#built-in-web-templates. See Figure 5-3.

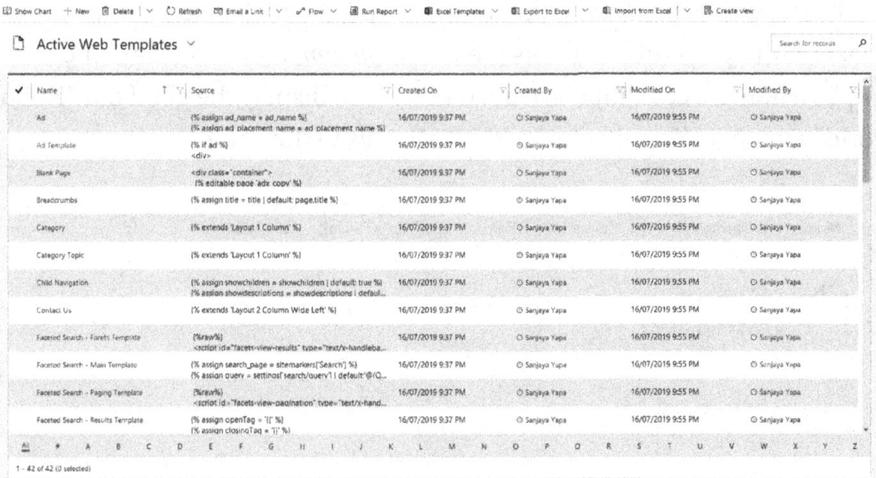

Figure 5-3. *Default web templates list*

Web Template Example

Before you continue, let's look at a quick example to see how you can create and use a web template. Navigate to the web templates section of the portal navigation and click New. Specify the settings shown in Figure 5-4 and enter the source code shown in Listing 5-1. You can see that the code editor comes with IntelliSense.

Listing 5-1. Sample Code Snippet for web template - Hello world example

```
{% if page.title contains "Custom"%}
    <h3>Hello from Custom Portal</h3>
{% else %}
    <h3>Hello world.</h3>
{% endif %}
```

This code simply checks the title of the page and displays some output. That is, if the page title contains the word *Custom*, then it displays the output when the condition is true. If not, it will display the good old "Hello world" message. You also can add HTML tags to the code.

Figure 5-4. *New web template*

Save and close the web template. The next step is to create a page template. The page template is the pointer to locate the actual template. To create the page template, navigate to Page Templates and click New. As you can see, on this screen you should make sure to change Type to Web Template, which will change the form to select the web template you have just created. Leave the rest as it is and click Save. Figure 5-5.

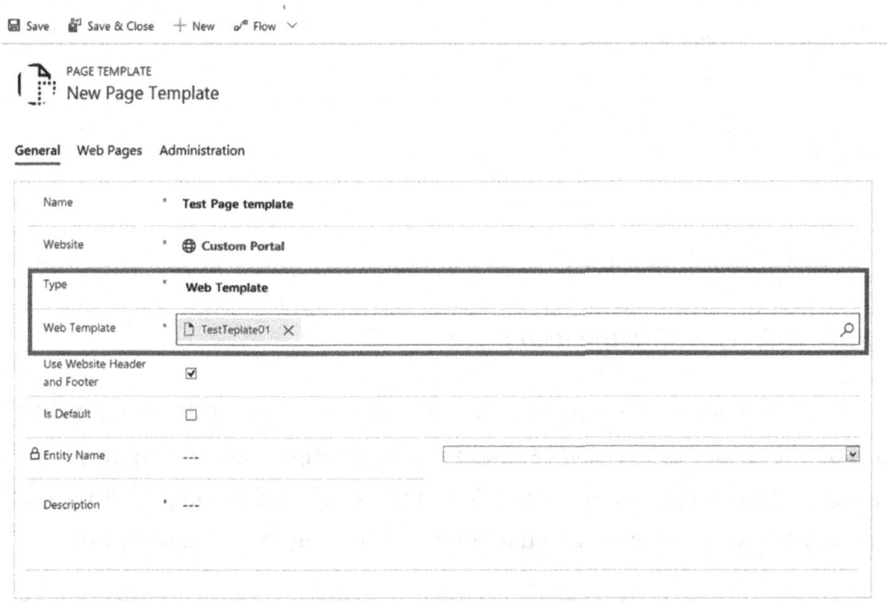

Figure 5-5. *Creating a page template*

Now to render all these to the portal, you should create a web page. Navigate to the web page section and click +New. Add the settings illustrated in Figure 5-6. Since you are not using any web forms, entity forms, or entity lists, leave those fields blank.

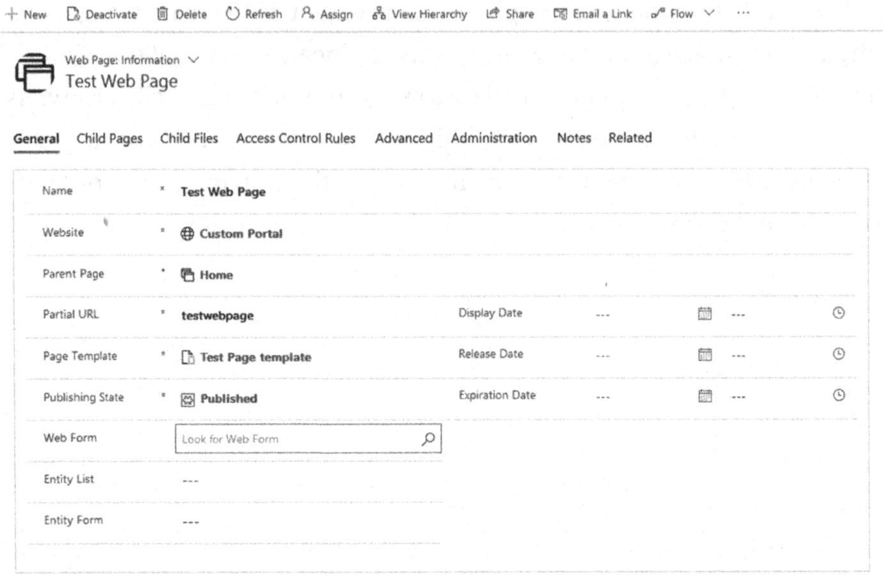

Figure 5-6. *Creating the web page*

Now, navigate to the URL. In this example, it is `https://sbmamembership. microsoftcrmportals.com/testwebpage/`. Change it according to your example. As you can see in Figure 5-7, it uses the default page header and footer, since you are opting to use it when creating the page template.

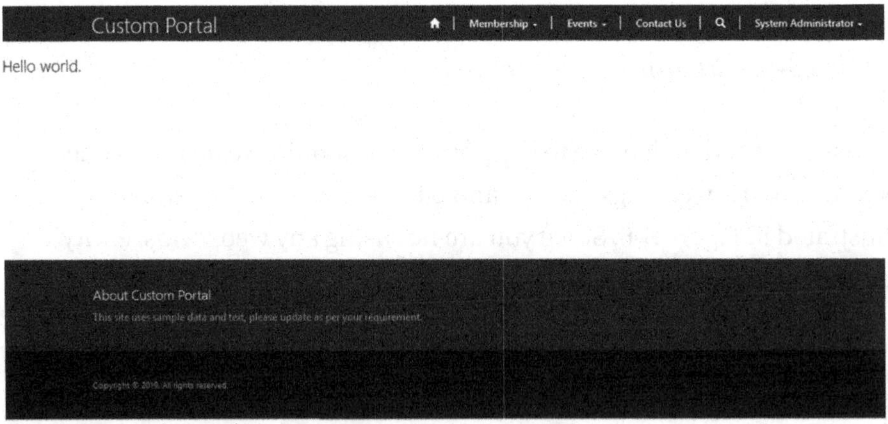

Figure 5-7. *Rendered web page*

Liquid Types

Like other programming language, Liquid has types. Liquid objects can return one of seven types: strings, Booleans, arrays, numbers, dictionaries, date/times, and nulls. The Assign and Capture tags are used to initialize Liquid variables.

String

A string is declared by using single or double quotes, as shown in Listing 5-2.

Listing 5-2. String Declaration

```
{% assign string_val1 = "Hello Dynamics 365 Portals" %}
<h2><b>{{string_val1}}</b></h2>

<br>
{% assign string_val1 = 'Single quotes for liquid strings' %}
<h3><b>{{string_val1}}</b></h3>
```

In Listing 5-2, the assign tag is used to assign the string value to the string variable. To display the string value, the {{ <value> }} syntax is used. Refresh the page and you will see output like in Figure 5-8.

Figure 5-8. *String variable output*

Number

A number variable declaration follows the same pattern and can be an integers or a float. Listing 5-3 shows how to declare number variables.

Listing 5-3. Numbers and Floats

```
<br>
<h3>Numbers and Floats</h3>
{% assign float_value = 9.56 %}
<h4>{{float_value}}</h4>
{% assign number_value = 120 %}
<h4>{{number_value}}</h4>
```

Boolean

Similar to the Boolean type you already know, this type can be either true or false. Listing 5-4 shows the declaration and use of Boolean variables.

Listing 5-4. Boolean

```
<br>
<h3>Boolean</h3>
{% assign bool_1 = true %}
{% assign bool_2 = false %}
{% if bool_1 %}
    <h4>bool_1 is true</h4>
{% endif %}
```

Figure 5-9 illustrates the output of both numbers and Boolean values.

Figure 5-9. *Numbers and Boolean output*

Date/Time

The date/time type is used to define specific date/time values (see Listing 5-5 and Figure 5-10).

Listing 5-5. Date/Time Type

```
<br>
<center><h3>Date and Time</h3></center>
{% assign NowDate = {now|date: 'g'} %}
{% assign NowDateFormatted = {now|date: 'MMMM dd, yyyy'} %}
<center><h4><b>{{NowDate}}</b></h4></center>
<center><h4><b>{{NowDateFormatted}}</b></h4></center>
```

Figure 5-10. *Date/time type*

Null

Null is used to embody an empty value, and any output returning a null value will render nothing. From a conditional logic standpoint, it will be treated as false.

Arrays

Arrays are used to hold a list of values. Like most other programming languages, Liquid arrays are zero-based. You can iterate the list using the for tag, and the length of the array can be returned by using the size attribute (see Listing 5-6).

Note   There is no specific way of initializing an array with Liquid. But you can use the split filter to filter a list of values in a variable. When the values are split, the variable will be treated as an array. Generally, in the Dynamics 365 world, you will be using arrays to hold existing lists, such as entity lists.

Listing 5-6. Arrays

```
{% assign string_val1 = "Hello Dynamics 365 Portals" %}
<center><h2><b>{{string_val1}}</b></h2></center>

<br>
<center><h3>Arrays</h3></center>
{% assign fellowShip = "Frodo, Sam, Merry, Pippin, Arragon,
Gandolf, Gimly, Legolas" | split: "," %}
{% for member in fellowShip %}
  <center><br>{{ member }}</center>
{% endfor %}
```

```
<br>
<center><h4>Access elements using index: Index 4 is - {{
fellowShip[4] }}</h4></center>

{% if fellowShip.size > 0 %}
  <center><h4>This array has {{ fellowShip.size }} elements.
  </h4></center>
{% endif %}
```

The output should look something like Figure 5-11.

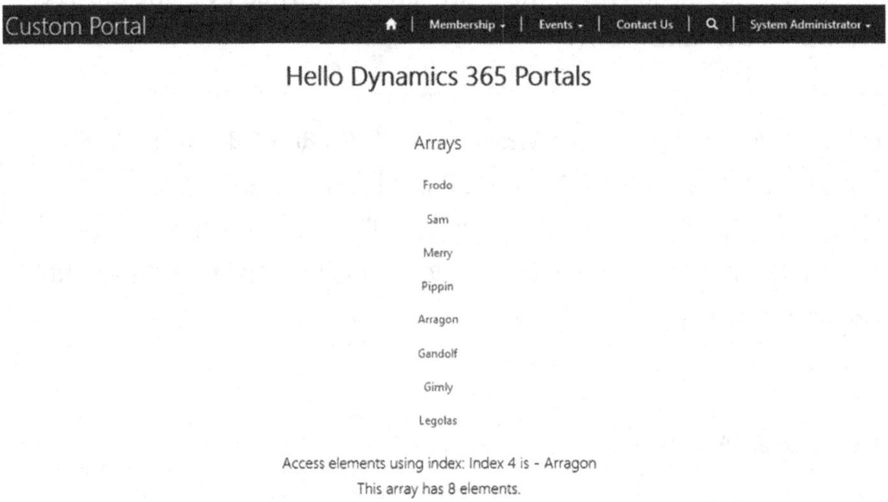

Figure 5-11. *Arrays*

Dictionaries

This type of list is capable of holding a list of values, and the values can be accessed by using a string key and iterating over the elements using the for tag. Generally, you will be using dictionaries to manipulate entity lists (see Listing 5-7).

Listing 5-7. Dictionary

```
<br>
<center><h3>Dictionary</h3></center>
{% assign eventList = entities['sbma_event'] %}

{% for item in eventList %}
  <br>{{ item }}
{% endfor %}
```

Liquid Operators

Liquid also has operators that can be used with `if` and `unless`. The following are the basic operators:

`==`	Equal
`!=`	Not equal
`or`	Logical or
`and`	Logical and
`>`	Greater than
`<`	Less than
`>=`	Greater than or equal to
`<=`	Less than or equal to
`Contains`	Tests the existence of a substring within a string
`startswith`	Checks whether a string starts with the given string
`endswith`	Checks whether a string ends with the given string

Conditions

Conditional statements are implemented using if, unless, and elseif/ else. The following code listings illustrate the use of these constructs in Liquid.

If Condition

This is the if condition that you probably already know.

```
{% if events.title == "Annual Dinner" %}
<h3>Everyone will be there!</h3>
{% endif %}
```

Unless

The unless condition is the reverse of the if condition. That is, if a certain condition is not met, then the code block will be executed.

```
{% unless eventsList.rating == "Good" %}
Then the event is not good.
{% endunless %}
```

Else/Else If

This can be used with if and unless statements. Traditionally, statements in an else block will be executed when the if condition is false. Also, with else if, you can combine multiple conditions like with traditional else if statements.

```
{% if contact.username == "JamesB" %}
Hey James Bond!
{% elsif contact.username == "administrator" %}
```

```
Hey Administrator!
{% else %}
Hi Stranger!
{% endif %}
```

Switch Statements

To implement switch statements, you can use case/when that initializes the switch statement.

```
{% assign personType = "Hobbit" %}
{% case personName %}
{% when "Hobbit" %}
This is a Hobbit
{% when "Wizard" %}
This is a Wizard
{% when "Man" %}
This is a Man
{% else %}
This is an Ork.
{% endcase %}
```

Note   When using conditional statements, some values are treated as true, and some are treated as false. For instance, null and Boolean false are treated as false, and empty strings, arrays, etc., are treated as true. For more information, visit https://docs.microsoft. com/en-us/dynamics365/customer-engagement/portals/ liquid-conditional-operators#summary.

Iterations

Like with other programming languages, iterations make a block of code execute repeatedly.

For

Similar to the `foreach` loop in C#, a `for` block of code is executed for the full list of available attributes.

```
{% for event in collection.eventList %}
{{ event.title }}
{% endfor %}
```

For further reading, please visit https://docs.microsoft.com/en-us/dynamics365/customer-engagement/portals/iteration-tags.

Liquid Objects

Liquid objects are used to output dynamic content to the page. All these objects contain attributes that can be accessed using the dot operator. For instance, the page object contains an attribute called `title` to access the title of the page. See Figure 5-12.

```
<center><h2><b>Page title is: {{ page.title }}</b></h2></center>
```

Hello Dynamics 365 Portals

Page title is: Test Web Page

Figure 5-12.   *Page object and the title attribute*

Entities

This object allows you to retrieve a Dynamics 365 CE entity by using the logical name of the entity. Listing 5-8 shows how to access the entity from the entities using the entity logical name.

Listing 5-8. Access Entity Properties

```
{% assign string_val1 = "Hello Dynamics 365 Portals" %}
<center><h2><b>{{string_val1}}</b></h2></center>

<center><h2><b>Page title  is: {{ page.title }}</b></h2></center>

{% assign sbmaEvent = entities.['sbma_event'] %}
{% if sbmaEvent %}
  <center><h3><b>Entity Logical Name:  {{ sbmaEvent.logical_
  name }} </b></h3></center>
{% endif %}
```

For further reading, visit https://docs.microsoft.com/en-us/ dynamics365/customer-engagement/portals/liquid-objects#entities.

Forloop

This object contains properties that can be used within a for loop. Keep in mind that this object can be used only inside the for loop. Listing 5-9 iterates through the list of child pages. It uses the forloop.first and forloop.index properties.

Listing 5-9. Forloop Properties

```
<center><h2><b>Page titiel is: {{ page.title }}</b></h2></center>

{% for child in page.children %}
{% if forloop.first %}
```

```
<center><h4><b>Child Page Title: {{ child.title }}</b></h4>
</center>
<center><h4><b>This is the first child page!</b></h4></center>
{% else %}
<center><h4><b>Child Page Title: {{ child.title }}</b></h4>
</center>
<center><h4><b>This is child page number {{ forloop.index }}.
</b></h4></center>
{% endif %}
{% endfor %}
```

Figure 5-13 shows the output of this code.

Figure 5-13. *For loop properties rendered*

Page

This object refers to the current portal page, and it provides access to breadcrumbs, titles, or URLs. Also, attributes relate to the entities of the current request. The following page has a nice example that you can directly copy into a web template and test it: `https://docs.microsoft.com/en-us/dynamics365/customer-engagement/portals/liquid-objects#page`. See Figure 5-14.

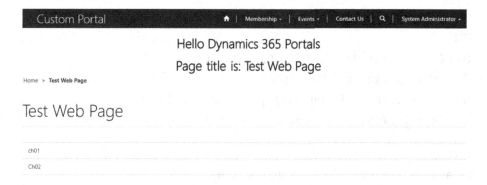

Figure 5-14. *Using a page object*

You can find the full list of these objects at https://docs.microsoft.
com/en-us/dynamics365/customer-engagement/portals/liquid-objects.

Filters

These are simple functions that are used to modify the output of variables
and objects. A filter is separated from the value it is applied to by |. Some
of these filters are capable of accepting parameters. There are filters for
arrays, dates, entity lists, math, strings, etc. In this section, we will explore a
few these filters to get familiarize with the usage.

String Filters

Listing 5-10 demonstrates the use of append, capitalize, downcase, and
replace. These filters are straightforward, and the use of each filter can be
determined by the name.

Listing 5-10. String Filters

```
{% assign string_val1 = "Hello Dynamics 365 Portals" %}
<center><h2><b>{{string_val1}}</b></h2></center>
```

```
<center><h2><b>Page title is: {{ page.title }}</b></h2></center>
<br>
<center><h3>String Filters</h3></center>
{% assign string_val2 = "Append Filter: " %}
<center><h4><b>{{string_val2 | append: 'This text is
appended'}}</b></h4></center>

<br>
{% assign string_val2 = "Capitalizing : " %}
<center><h4><b>{{string_val2 | capitalize }}</b></h4></center>

<br>
{% assign string_val2 = "DOWNCASE TEXT : " %}
<center><h4><b>{{string_val2 | downcase }}</b></h4></center>

<br>
{% assign string_val2 = "Replace text : " %}
<center><h4><b>{{string_val2}} {{"Dynamics 365 portals" |
replace: 'portals', 'Liquid Templates' }}</b></h4></center>
```

Figure 5-15 shows the output of the code.

Figure 5-15. *String filters*

Math Filters

These filters are for performing mathematical operations on the output. Listing 5-11 demonstrates the use of the available math operators. As you can see from this example, there are a few options for rounding operations. The floor filter will round down the value to the nearest integer, whereas the round filter can be used to round a value to the nearest integer, or you can specify the number of decimals, as shown in the code.

Listing 5-11. Math Filters

```
 {% assign string_val1 = "Hello Dynamics 365 Portals" %}
<center><h2><b>{{string_val1}}</b></h2></center>

<center><h2><b>Page title is: {{ page.title }}</b></h2></center>
<br>
<center><h3>Math Filters</h3></center>
{% assign string_val2 = "Math operation (150 * 2 -5 / 3): " %}
<center><h4><b>{{string_val2}} {{150 | time:2 | minus:5 |
devided_by: 3}}</b></h4></center>

<br>
{% assign string_val2 = "Rounding 32.59 : " %}
<center><h4><b>{{string_val2}} {{32.59 | ceil }}</b></h4></center>

<br>
{% assign string_val2 = "Floor 32.25 : " %}
<center><h4><b>{{string_val2}} {{32.25 | floor }}</b></h4></center>

<br>
{% assign string_val2 = "Round 45.6578 : " %}
<center><h4><b>{{string_val2}} {{45.6578 | round: 2}}</b></h4>
</center>
```

Figure 5-16 shows the output of the code.

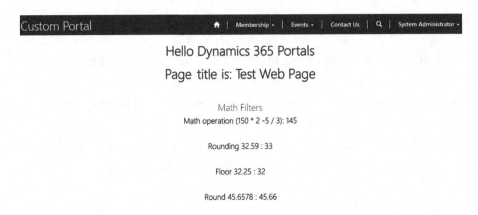

Figure 5-16. *Math filters*

Date Filters

The date filters are used to apply a format to the output or perform arithmetic operations on the output. See Listing 5-12.

Listing 5-12. Date Filters

```
{% assign string_val1 = "Hello Dynamics 365 Portals" %}
<center><h2><b>{{string_val1}}</b></h2></center>

<center><h2><b>Page titiel is: {{ page.title }}</b></h2></center>
<br>
<center><h3>Date Filters</h3></center>
{% assign string_val2 = "Now Date: " %}
<center><h4><b>{{string_val2}} {{now | date : 'g'}}</b></h4></center>
<center><h4><b>{{'Now Date (Formatted) '}} {{now | date : 'MMMM
dd, yyyy'}}</b></h4></center>

<br>
<center><h4><b>{{'Now: '}} {{now | date : 'g'}}</b></h4></center>
<center><h4><b>{{'Add 1 day to Now: '}} {{now | date_add_days :
1}}</b></h4></center>
```

192

```
<center><h4><b>{{'Minus three and half days: '}} {{now | date_
add_days : -3.5}}</b></h4></center>

<br>
<center><h4><b>{{'Now: '}} {{now | date : 'g'}}</b></h4></center>
<center><h4><b>{{'Add 1 Month to Now: '}} {{now | date_add_
months : 1}}</b></h4></center>
<center><h4><b>{{'Minus three Months: '}} {{now | date_add_
months : -3}}</b></h4></center>

<br>
<center><h4><b>{{'Now: '}} {{now | date : 'g'}}</b></h4></center>
<center><h4><b>{{'Format date to ISO 8601: '}} {{now | date_to_
iso8601}}</b></h4></center>
<center><h4><b>{{'Format date to RFS 822: '}} {{now | date_to_
rfc822}}</b></h4></center>
```

Figure 5-17 shows the output for the code.

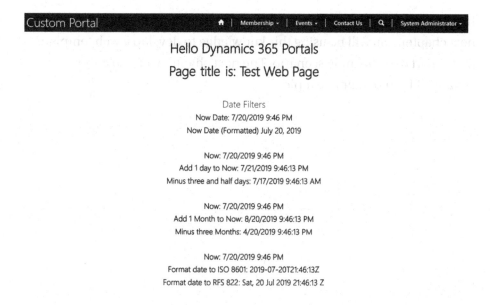

Figure 5-17. *Date filters*

There are more filters available, and you will be looking at filters such as array filters and entity list filters when working with the advanced templates in the next chapter. You can visit the following page for more information about filters: `https://docs.microsoft.com/en-us/dynamics365/customer-engagement/portals/liquid-filters`.

Important   Before moving to the next chapter, you should try the sample code given in these examples. You can easily create a web template and add the code as explained. You should especially try using Liquid conditions, iterations, objects, and filters.

There are even more examples in the Microsoft documentation that you should spend some time trying.

Summary

In this chapter, you learned about the basics of Liquid templates. In the next chapter, you will be using this knowledge to develop a web template that is part of the sample scenario. The next chapter will also cover advanced Liquid template topics.

CHAPTER 6

Advanced Liquid Templates

In the previous chapter you learned about the basics of Liquid templates. In this chapter, I cover the advanced topics and provide you with a guide to create a custom web page. I discuss topics such as retrieving a single record and multiple records, using include tags and entity list tags, retrieving records using FetchXml, and creating conditional entity forms. I also give you guidelines for best practices. Let's dive deep into the examples, starting with retrieving data.

Retrieving Data

In this example, we will be retrieving details of the records in an entity list. For this, we will be using the event list created in one of the previous examples, as shown in Figure 6-1.

© Sanjaya Yapa 2019
S. Yapa, *Getting Started with Dynamics 365 Portals*,
https://doi.org/10.1007/978-1-4842-5346-5_6

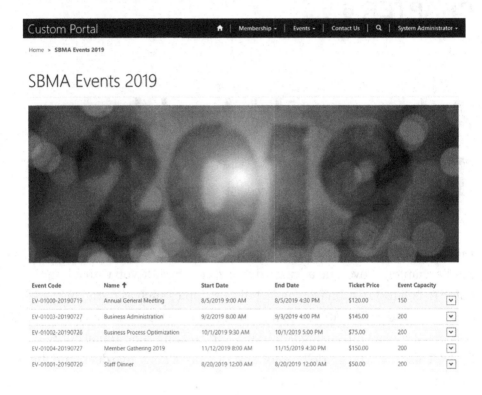

Figure 6-1. *Event list shown in entity list*

The functionality we want is to show the Event Details when the Event Code link is clicked. To pull up the details of the record, you must know the GUID of the record.

Step 1: Create the Web Template

As explained in Chapter 5, you need to create a web template to display the details of the event. Figure 6-2 illustrates the new web template. As you can see, the Liquid code is embedded in HTML. Most of the code listed in this example was explained in Chapter 5.

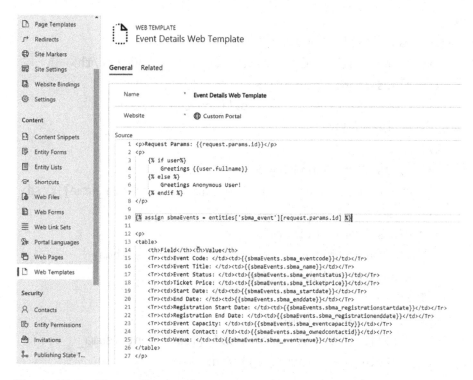

Figure 6-2. New web template

```
<div class="container">
<p>Request Params: {{request.params.id}}</p>
<p>
    {% if user%}
        Greetings {{user.fullname}}
    {% else %}
        Greetings Anonymous User!
    {% endif %}
</p>

{% assign sbmaEvents = entities['sbma_event'][request.params.id] %}
```

```
<p>
<table class="table table-hover">
    <th scope="col">Field</th><th scope="col">Value</th>
    <Tr class="table-primary">
        <td>Event Code: </td><td>{{sbmaEvents.sbma_
        eventcode}}</td>
    </Tr>
    <Tr class="table-primary">
        <td>Event Title: </td><td>{{sbmaEvents.sbma_name}}</td>
    </Tr>
    <Tr class="table-primary">
        <td>Event Status: </td><td>{{sbmaEvents.sbma_
        eventstatus.Label}}</td>
    </Tr>
    <Tr class="table-primary">
        <td>Ticket Price: </td><td>$ {{sbmaEvents.sbma_
        ticketprice | round: 2}}</td>
    </Tr>
    <Tr class="table-primary">
        <td>Start Date: </td><td>{{sbmaEvents.sbma_startdate |
        date_add_hours:10}}</td>
    </Tr>
    <Tr class="table-primary">
        <td>End Date: </td><td>{{sbmaEvents.sbma_enddate |
        date_add_hours:10}}</td>
    </Tr>
    <Tr class="table-primary">
        <td>Registration Start Date: </td><td>{{sbmaEvents.
        sbma_registrationstartdate | date_add_hours:10}}</td>
    </Tr>
```

```
<Tr class="table-primary">
    <td>Registration End Date: </td><td>{{sbmaEvents.sbma_
    registrationenddate | date_add_hours:10}}</td>
</Tr>
<Tr class="table-primary">
    <td>Event Capacity: </td><td>{{sbmaEvents.sbma_
    eventcapacity}}</td>
</Tr>
<Tr class="table-primary">
    <td>Event Contact: </td><td>{{sbmaEvents.sbma_
    ownedcontactid.Name}}</td>
</Tr>
<Tr class="table-primary">
    <td>Venue: </td><td>{{sbmaEvents.sbma_eventvenue.
    Name}}</td>
</Tr>
</table>
</div>
</p>
```

Note that the example is using the formatting of the default Bootstrap template.

Important   When setting an option's value, you should use the syntax given here:

```
<td>Event Status: </td><td>{{sbmaEvents.sbma_eventstatus.
Label}}</td>
```

When reading lookup values, you should use the following syntax:

```
<td>Event Contact: </td><td>{{sbmaEvents.sbma_ownedcontactid.
Name}}</td>
```

In Liquid, most entity attributes are mapped directly, but some are returned as objects. You can find more information at `https://docs.microsoft.com/en-us/dynamics365/customer-engagement/portals/liquid-objects#entity`.

Step 2: Create the Page Template

This is where you are going to glue your template to a web page. Go to the Page Template page and create a new page template, as shown in Figure 6-3.

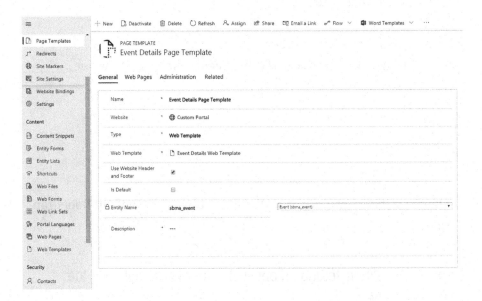

Figure 6-3. *New page template*

Step 3: Create the Web Page

The next step is to create the web page and bind the web template using the page template. See Figure 6-4.

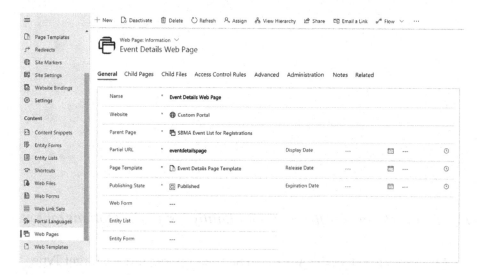

Figure 6-4. *Creating a web page for the event details page*

Step 4: Update the Entity List Details Options

The final step is to update the Entity Lists Details section on the Options tab. As shown in Figure 6-5, change the settings of the Details page to redirect to the new web page created.

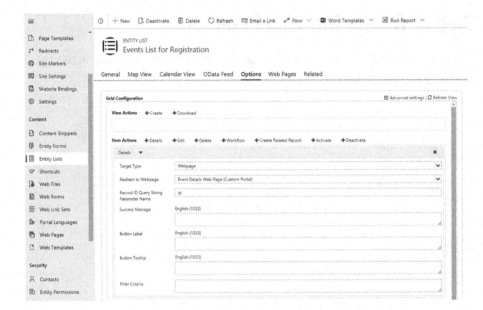

Figure 6-5. *Detail Form settings for Entitiy List under Options tabs*

Make sure to select the Advanced Settings option and set Target Type to Webpage. Then set the Redirect Webpage setting to the new web page created. To load the record, you must fill in the Record ID Query String Parameter Name field, which will be passed to the request and will return the selected record. Save the settings and test the configuration. When you click the event link, the event ID is passed to the request, and the data is retrieved, as shown in Figure 6-6.

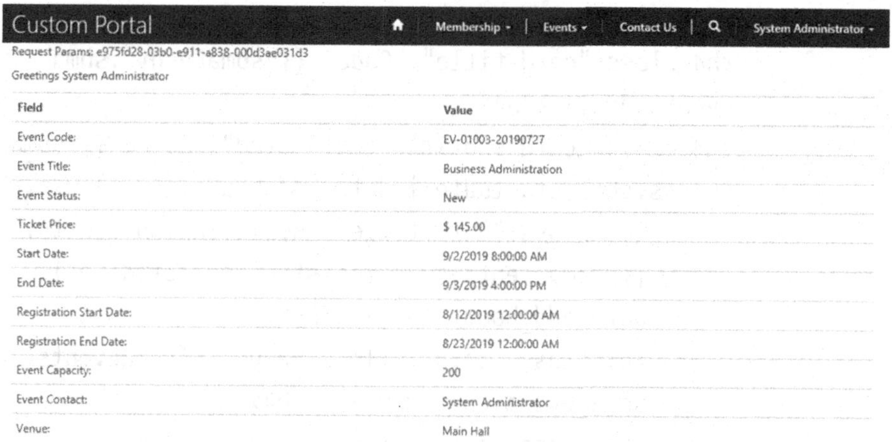

Figure 6-6. *Custom event details window*

Retrieving Multiple Records

In this example, you will learn how to retrieve multiple records and format the results using the default Bootstrap theme. Our objective here is to display the events list in a more interesting way to the user. To begin, let's create a web template and add the following code to it:

```
<div class="container">
  <div class="page-heading">
      {%include 'breadcrumbs' %}
  </div>
  {% include 'page_header'%}
  {% include 'page_copy' %}
  {% entitylist id:page.adx_entitylist.id %}
   {% entityview logical_name:'sbma_event',name:'Active Events
   View',page_size:10 %}
     {% for sbmaEvents in entityview.records %}
       <div class="card mb-3">
         <h2 class="card-header"> {{ sbmaEvents.sbma_name }} </h2>
```

```
            <div class="card-body">
              <h4 class="card-title"> Code: {{ sbmaEvents.sbma_
              eventcode }} </h4>
              <h4 class="card-subtitle text-muted"> Date: {{ sbma
              Events.sbma_startdate | date_add_hours:10  }} </h4>
                    <h5 class="card-title"> Registration Starts:
                    {{ sbmaEvents.sbma_registrationstartdate |
                    date_add_hours:10 }} </h5>
                    <h4 class="card-title"> Venue: {{sbmaEvents.
                    sbma_eventvenue.Name}} </h4>
                    <h4 class="card-title text-muted"><b>
                    Tickets $: {{sbmaEvents.sbma_ticketprice |
                    round: 2 }} </b></h4>
          </div>
        </div>
    {% endfor %}
   {% endentityview %}
  {% endentitylist %}
</div>
```

This code is simply using the entity list that was assigned to the web page and iterating the results. This code line is reading the entity list of the web page:

```
{% entitylist id:page.adx_entitylist.id %}
```

Also, the code refers to the view attached to the entity list in the following code line:

```
{% entityview logical_name:'sbma_event',name:'Active Events
View',page_size:10 %}
```

In the next line, the retrieved records will be iterated using the for block, and you can see that some of the default Bootstrap formatting is applied.

Important   In this code sample, you can see that when displaying the event dates, ten hours are added to the date. The reason for this is that when Dynamics 365 CE stores data, it stores it in UTC format. So, when you retrieve the values in a portal, it might show an incorrect date. As per the following blog article, this is the quick fix, but it might not be the correct answer for the countries that use daylight saving time. Please refer to the following page for more information: `http://himbap.com/blog/?p=3493`.

The rest of the code is pure Liquid code, so save the web template.

The next step is to create the page template like you did earlier. You should make sure the page template is referring to the web template that you have created. Finally, create the web page, which is also same as before. Make sure it is referring to the correct page template.

Important   When you create the entity list, you must make sure to add the columns to the view you will be using in the page. For this example, a new view was created that includes all the required columns, as shown in Figure 6-7. In other words, when you write a SQL query, you should include all the columns that you are planning to manipulate. The same principle applies here.

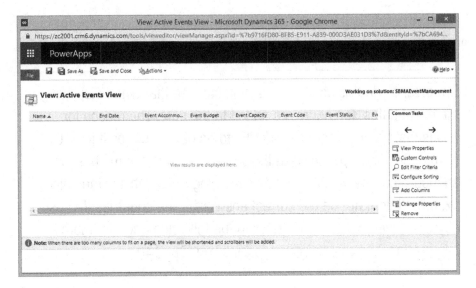

Figure 6-7. *View of the portal entity list*

In the entity list, select the newly created view and make sure your Liquid code references the list as explained previously. See Figure 6-8.

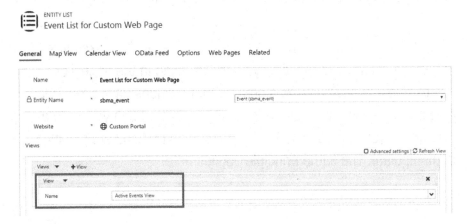

Figure 6-8. *Selecting the new view created for the entity list*

Save the settings and navigate to the new web page created from the portal. Your output should look something like Figure 6-9.

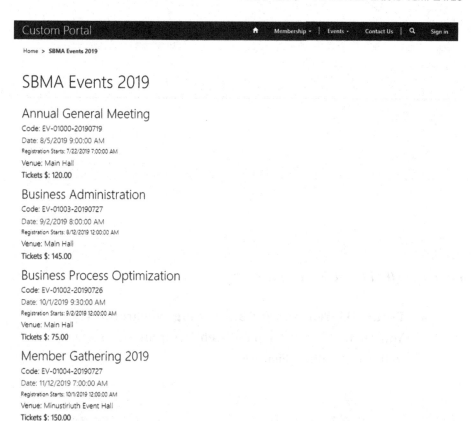

Figure 6-9. *List of events shown in the portal*

Using XrmToolBox for Portals

XrmToolBox provides a few tools that can be used to manage portals. You can download XrmToolBox from https://www.xrmtoolbox.com.

- **Portal 365 Duplicator**: This tool is for creating a complete copy of the portal configuration with new primary keys. The references are also updated accordingly. Then it can be imported to a completely new environment (Figure 6-10).

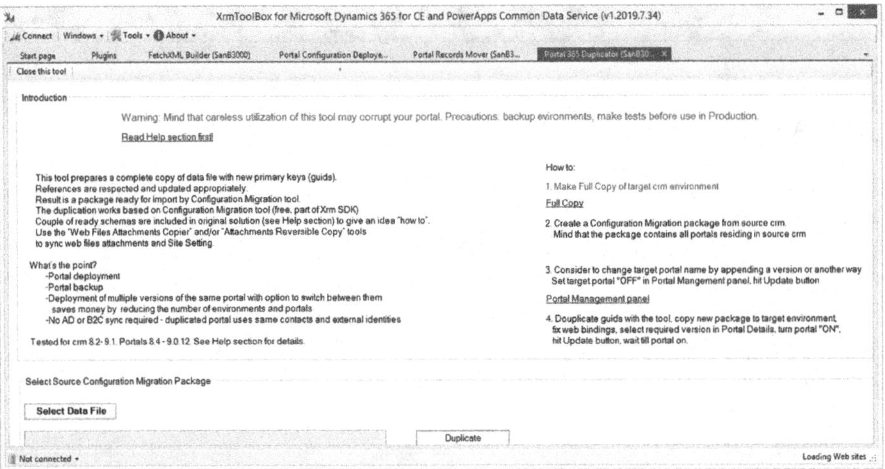

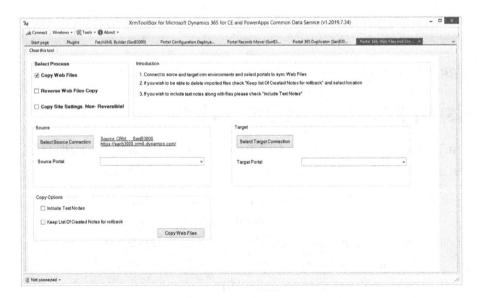

Figure 6-10. *Portal 365 Duplicator*

- **Portal 365 Web Files and Site Setting Synchronizer**:
  You can use this tool to move web files from the source
  to the destination (Figure 6-11).

Figure 6-11. *Portal 365 Web Files and Site Setting Synchronizer*

- **Portal Code Editor**: Out of all these tools, Portal Code Editor is a handy tool to edit Liquid code. As shown in Figure 6-12, you can easily access and edit the code.

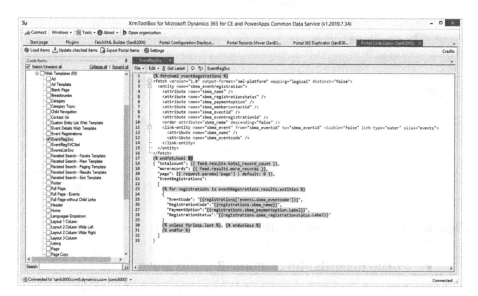

Figure 6-12. *Portal Code Editor*

- **Portal Configuration Compare**: You can use this tool to compare the configuration in two environments (Figure 6-13).

Figure 6-13. *Portal Configuration Compare*

- **Portal Records Mover**: Portal Records Mover is for moving configuration records from one environment to another. See the section "Deploying Portal Files" later in this chapter for more information.

- **Portal Configuration Deployer**: This is ideal for deploying selected configurations, and you can find more details about the plug-in in the section "Deploying Portal Files" later in this chapter.

- **Portal Web File Explorer**: You can use this plug-in to explore the portal folder structure and add any web files required (Figure 6-14).

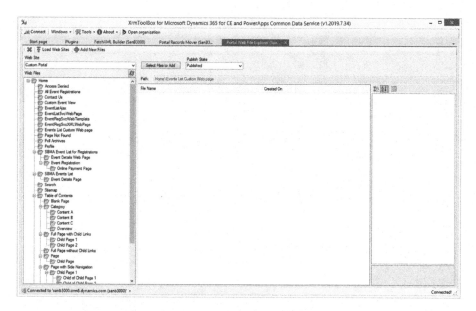

Figure 6-14. *Portal Web File Explorer*

- **Portal Webform Cloner**: This plug-in can be used
  to clone or copy existing web forms. It's useful in
  scenarios where you must create web forms in different
  scenarios, for instance, create and update operations
  (Figure 6-15).

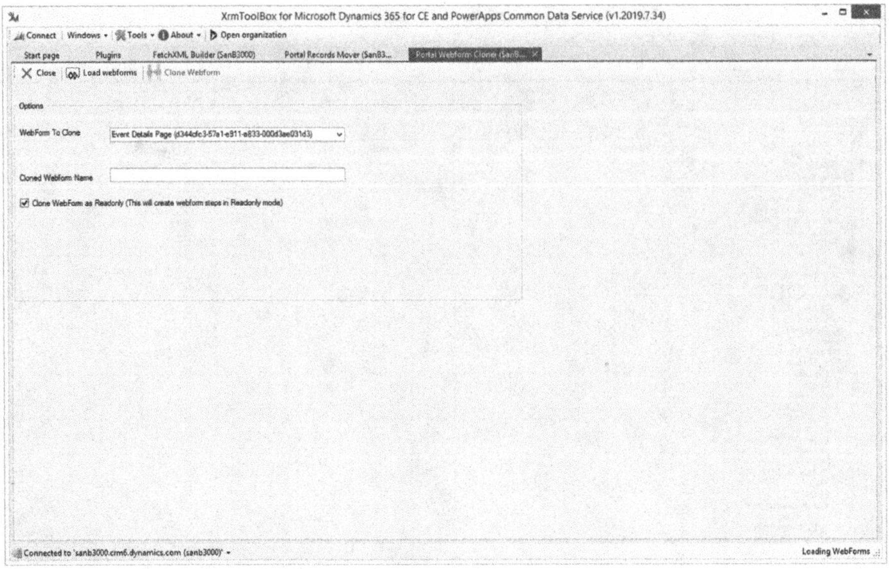

Figure 6-15. *Portal Webform Cloner*

When you add more and more customizations to meet client requirements, these tools will become very handy to manage all these complex changes.

Navigating to the Details of the Event

Now that we have loaded the event list in a custom way, the next step is to load the details from this page. We will be modifying the code that we used in the previous example to load the details page.

```
<div class="container">
    <div class="page-heading">
        {%include 'breadcrumbs' %}
    </div>
    {% include 'page_header'%}
    {% include 'page_copy' %}
```

```
{% entitylist id:page.adx_entitylist.id %}
 {% entityview logical_name:'sbma_event',name:'Active
 Events List',page_size:10 %}
  {% for sbmaEvents in entityview.records %}
    <div class="card mb-3">
     <h2 class="card-header"> {{ sbmaEvents.sbma_name }} </h2>
     <div class="card-body">
       <a class= "btn btn-default btn-xs"
          href="{{ entitylist.detail_url}}?{{entitylist.
          detail_id_parameter}}={{sbmaEvents.id}}"
          title="{{ entitylist.detail_label }}">
        <h4 class="card-title"> Code: {{ sbmaEvents.sbma_
        eventcode }} </h4>
       </a>
           <h4 class="card-subtitle text-muted">
           Date: {{ sbmaEvents.sbma_startdate | date_add_
           hours:10  }} </h4>
           <h5 class="card-title"> Registration Starts: {{
           sbmaEvents.sbma_registrationstartdate | date_
           add_hours:10 }} </h5>
           <h4 class="card-title"> Venue: {{sbmaEvents.
           sbma_eventvenue.Name}} </h4>
           <h4 class="card-title text-muted"><b> Tickets $:
           {{sbmaEvents.sbma_ticketprice | round: 2 }}
           </b></h4>
      </div>
    </div>
  {% endfor %}
 {% endentityview %}
{% endentitylist %}
</div>
```

The highlighted lines illustrate the changes to code that will open the details Page. This is basically passing the record ID as a query string parameter using a Bootstrap-style hyperlink, which will open the details Page. For this to successfully work, you must enable the details Page for the entity list on the Options tab. Then this code will use the nominated page to load the details. See Figure 6-16.

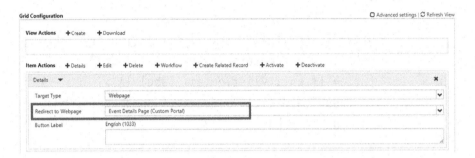

Figure 6-16. *Event Details Page set for the entity list*

Now, when you navigate to the event list, you can see the event code is highlighted, which will be used as the link to the Event Details page. See Figure 6-17.

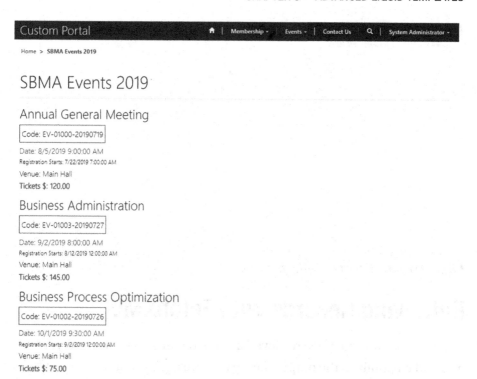

Figure 6-17. *Event code is highlighted as the link to the event details*

When the user clicks the event code on this page, the user can navigate to the event details page, as shown in Figure 6-18. Note that we have used the same event details page that we created for the single-record example.

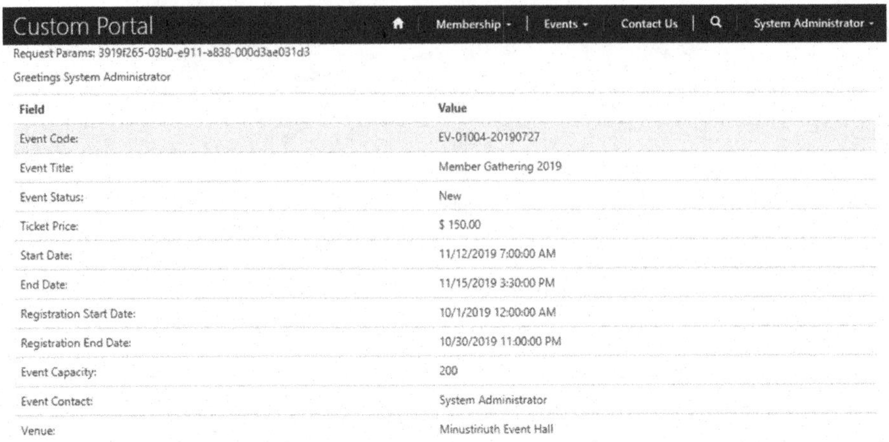

Figure 6-18. *Event details displayed*

Retrieving Records with FetchXML

In the previous section, we retrieved a list of records using the entity
lists and customized the output. Entity lists are tightly bound with views,
and if you are presented with a complex scenario, then you will end up
writing multiple views. This is a not a good practice because it can lead to
maintenance overhead. In such situations, FetchXML will save the day for
you. That is, you can easily create a FetchXML query with either Advanced
Find view or the FetchXML Builder of XrmToolBox.

Let's start with simply retrieving the event registrations. In
this example, we will be retrieving all the event registrations using
FetchXML. The following is the FetchXML query:

```
<fetch version="1.0" output-format="xml-platform"
mapping="logical" distinct="false">
  <entity name="sbma_eventregistration">
    <attribute name="sbma_name" />
    <attribute name="sbma_registrationstatus" />
    <attribute name="sbma_paymentoption" />
```

```
      <attribute name="sbma_membercontactid" />
      <attribute name="sbma_eventid" />
      <attribute name="sbma_eventregistrationid" />
      <order attribute="sbma_name" descending="false" />
    </entity>
</fetch>
```

As mentioned earlier, this query was taken from the Advanced Find view. Let's create the web template and add the Liquid code to the previous FetchXML query. Here we have used the FetchXML tag to include the query. We are just querying the Event Registration list and adding some HTML formatting to the table.

```
<div class="container">
  <div class="page-heading">
    {% include 'breadcrumbs' %}
  </div>
  {% include 'page_header' %}
  {% include 'page_copy' %}
  {% fetchxml eventRegistrations %}
  <fetch version="1.0" output-format="xml-platform"
  mapping="logical" distinct="false">
    <entity name="sbma_eventregistration">
      <attribute name="sbma_name" />
      <attribute name="sbma_registrationstatus" />
      <attribute name="sbma_paymentoption" />
      <attribute name="sbma_membercontactid" />
      <attribute name="sbma_eventid" />
      <attribute name="sbma_eventregistrationid" />
      <order attribute="sbma_name" descending="false" />
    </entity>
  </fetch>
  {% endfetchxml %}
```

```
<table class="table table-hover">
  <tr>
      <th scope="col">Account Name</th>
      <th scope="col">Event</th>
      <th scope="col">Member Contact</th>
      <th scope="col">Payment Option</th>
      <th scope="col">Registration Status</th>
    </tr>
  </thead>
  <tbody>
      {% for fetchResult in eventRegistrations.results.
      entities %}
      <tr>
          <td>{{fetchResult.sbma_name}}</td>
          <td>{{fetchResult.sbma_eventid.Name}}</td>
          <td>{{fetchResult.sbma_membercontactid.Name}}</td>
          <td>{{fetchResult.sbma_paymentoption.Label}}</td>
          <td>{{fetchResult.sbma_registrationstatus.Label}}
          </td>
        </tr>
      {% endfor %}
    </tbody>
  </table>
</div>
```

Save the web template and create the page template and finally the web page. The page looks like Figure 6-19.

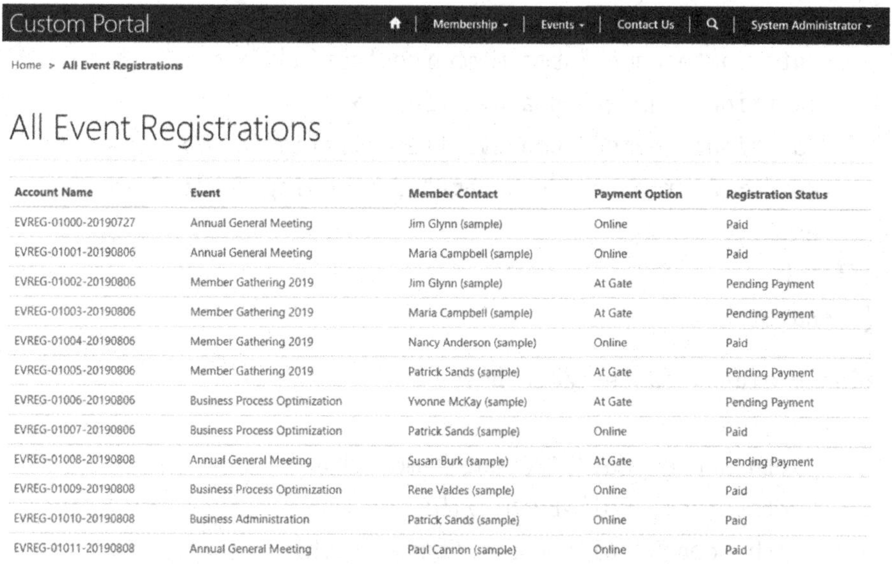

Account Name	Event	Member Contact	Payment Option	Registration Status
EVREG-01000-20190727	Annual General Meeting	Jim Glynn (sample)	Online	Paid
EVREG-01001-20190806	Annual General Meeting	Maria Campbell (sample)	Online	Paid
EVREG-01002-20190806	Member Gathering 2019	Jim Glynn (sample)	At Gate	Pending Payment
EVREG-01003-20190806	Member Gathering 2019	Maria Campbell (sample)	At Gate	Pending Payment
EVREG-01004-20190806	Member Gathering 2019	Nancy Anderson (sample)	Online	Paid
EVREG-01005-20190806	Member Gathering 2019	Patrick Sands (sample)	At Gate	Pending Payment
EVREG-01006-20190806	Business Process Optimization	Yvonne McKay (sample)	At Gate	Pending Payment
EVREG-01007-20190806	Business Process Optimization	Patrick Sands (sample)	Online	Paid
EVREG-01008-20190808	Annual General Meeting	Susan Burk (sample)	At Gate	Pending Payment
EVREG-01009-20190808	Business Process Optimization	Rene Valdes (sample)	Online	Paid
EVREG-01010-20190808	Business Administration	Patrick Sands (sample)	Online	Paid
EVREG-01011-20190808	Annual General Meeting	Paul Cannon (sample)	Online	Paid

***Figure 6-19.** All Event Registrations table*

Now let's add some traffic light formatting based on the different statuses of the records. Let's highlight the paid registrations in light green and the pending registrations in light red. The following is the code:

```
<div class="container">
  <div class="page-heading">
    {% include 'breadcrumbs' %}
  </div>
  {% include 'page_header' %}
  {% include 'page_copy' %}
  {% fetchxml eventRegistrations %}
  <fetch version="1.0" output-format="xml-platform"
  mapping="logical" distinct="false">
    <entity name="sbma_eventregistration">
      <attribute name="sbma_name" />
      <attribute name="sbma_registrationstatus" />
```

```
        <attribute name="sbma_paymentoption" />
        <attribute name="sbma_membercontactid" />
        <attribute name="sbma_eventid" />
        <attribute name="sbma_eventregistrationid" />
        <order attribute="sbma_name" descending="false" />
    </entity>
</fetch>
{% endfetchxml %}

<table class="table table-hover">
    <tr>
        <th scope="col">Account Name</th>
        <th scope="col">Event</th>
        <th scope="col">Member Contact</th>
        <th scope="col">Payment Option</th>
        <th scope="col">Registration Status</th>
    </tr>
</thead>
<tbody>
    {% for fetchResult in eventRegistrations.results.
    entities %}
    <tr>
        <td>{{fetchResult.sbma_name}}</td>
        <td>{{fetchResult.sbma_eventid.Name}}</td>
        <td>{{fetchResult.sbma_membercontactid.Name}}</td>
        <td>{{fetchResult.sbma_paymentoption.Label}}</td>
        {%case fetchResult.sbma_registrationstatus.Label %}
        {% when "Paid" %}
          <td bgcolor="#99FF99">
                {{fetchResult.sbma_registrationstatus.
                Label}}</td>
```

```
      {% when "Pending Payment" %}
        <td bgcolor="#FF9999">
              {{fetchResult.sbma_registrationstatus.
              Label}}</td>
      {% else %}
        <td bgcolor="#FFCC99">
              {{fetchResult.sbma_registrationstatus.
              Label}}</td>
      {% endcase %}

    </tr>
    {% endfor %}
  </tbody>
  </table>
</div>
```

The highlighted code lines are an if/else statement where it's simple to change the color of the background of the cell based on the value. The output should look like Figure 6-20.

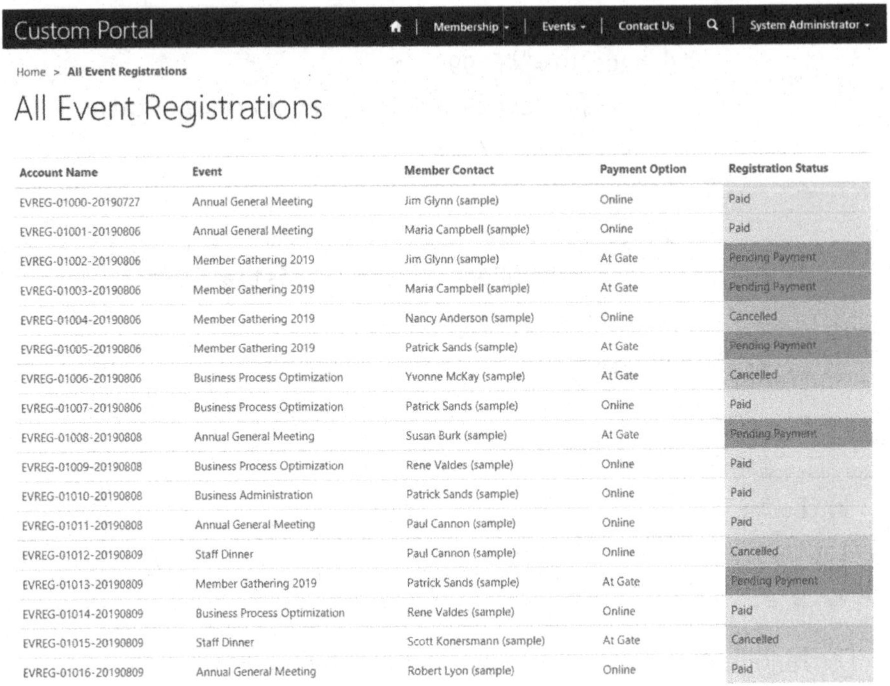

Figure 6-20. *Traffic lights effect*

Linked Entities

The following example demonstrates how to access the linked entities. In this example, we are going to show the event to which the registration belongs. The alias of the link tag of FetchXML is important here. As you can see from the highlighted code line, the alias is used to access the related entity record.

```
<div class="container">
  <div class="page-heading">
    {% include 'breadcrumbs' %}
  </div>
```

```
{% include 'page_header' %}
{% include 'page_copy' %}
{% fetchxml eventRegistrations %}
<fetch version="1.0" output-format="xml-platform"
mapping="logical" distinct="false">
<entity name="sbma_eventregistration">
  <attribute name="sbma_name" />
  <attribute name="sbma_registrationstatus" />
  <attribute name="sbma_paymentoption" />
  <attribute name="sbma_membercontactid" />
  <attribute name="sbma_eventid" />
  <attribute name="sbma_eventregistrationid" />
  <order attribute="sbma_name" descending="false" />
  <link-entity name="sbma_event" from="sbma_eventid"
  to="sbma_eventid" visible="false" link-type="outer"
  alias="events">
    <attribute name="sbma_name" />
    <attribute name="sbma_eventcode" />
  </link-entity>
</entity>
</fetch>
{% endfetchxml %}

<table id="dataTable" class="table table table-hover">
  <tr>
      <th scope="col">Event</th>
      <th scope="col">Registration Code</th>
      <th scope="col">Event</th>
      <th scope="col">Member Contact</th>
      <th scope="col">Payment Option</th>
      <th scope="col">Registration Status</th>
    </tr>
  </thead>
```

```
    <tbody>
        {% for fetchResult in eventRegistrations.results.entities %}
        <tr>
            <td>{{fetchResult['events.sbma_eventcode']}}</td>
            <td>{{fetchResult.sbma_name}}</td>
            <td>{{fetchResult.sbma_eventid.Name}}</td>
            <td>{{fetchResult.sbma_membercontactid.Name}}</td>
            <td>{{fetchResult.sbma_paymentoption.Label}}</td>
            {% if fetchResult.sbma_registrationstatus.Label ==
            "Paid" %}
              <td bgcolor="#99FF99">{{fetchResult.sbma_
              registrationstatus.Label}}</td>
            {% elseif fetchResult.sbma_registrationstatus.Label
            == "Pending Payment" %}
              <td bgcolor="#FF9999">{{fetchResult.sbma_
              registrationstatus.Label}}</td>
            {% else %}
              <td bgcolor="#FFCC99">{{fetchResult.sbma_
              registrationstatus.Label}}</td>
            {% endif %}
        </tr>
        {% endfor %}
    </tbody>
  </table>
</div>
```

Figure 6-21 shows what the output looks like.

Custom Portal				🏠 | Membership ▾ | Events ▾ | Contact Us | 🔍 | System Administrator ▾		

Home > **All Event Registrations**

All Event Registrations

Event	Registration Code	Event	Member Contact	Payment Option	Registration Status
EV-01000-20190719	EVREG-01000-20190727	Annual General Meeting	Jim Glynn (sample)	Online	Paid
EV-01000-20190719	EVREG-01001-20190806	Annual General Meeting	Maria Campbell (sample)	Online	Paid
EV-01004-20190727	EVREG-01002-20190806	Member Gathering 2019	Jim Glynn (sample)	At Gate	Pending Payment
EV-01004-20190727	EVREG-01003-20190806	Member Gathering 2019	Maria Campbell (sample)	At Gate	Pending Payment
EV-01004-20190727	EVREG-01004-20190806	Member Gathering 2019	Nancy Anderson (sample)	Online	Cancelled
EV-01004-20190727	EVREG-01005-20190806	Member Gathering 2019	Patrick Sands (sample)	At Gate	Pending Payment
EV-01002-20190726	EVREG-01006-20190806	Business Process Optimization	Yvonne McKay (sample)	At Gate	Cancelled
EV-01002-20190726	EVREG-01007-20190806	Business Process Optimization	Patrick Sands (sample)	Online	Paid
EV-01000-20190719	EVREG-01008-20190808	Annual General Meeting	Susan Burk (sample)	At Gate	Pending Payment
EV-01002-20190726	EVREG-01009-20190808	Business Process Optimization	Rene Valdes (sample)	Online	Paid
EV-01003-20190727	EVREG-01010-20190808	Business Administration	Patrick Sands (sample)	Online	Paid
EV-01000-20190719	EVREG-01011-20190808	Annual General Meeting	Paul Cannon (sample)	Online	Paid
EV-01001-20190720	EVREG-01012-20190809	Staff Dinner	Paul Cannon (sample)	Online	Cancelled
EV-01004-20190727	EVREG-01013-20190809	Member Gathering 2019	Patrick Sands (sample)	At Gate	Pending Payment
EV-01002-20190726	EVREG-01014-20190809	Business Process Optimization	Rene Valdes (sample)	Online	Paid
EV-01001-20190720	EVREG-01015-20190809	Staff Dinner	Scott Konersmann (sample)	At Gate	Cancelled
EV-01000-20190719	EVREG-01016-20190809	Annual General Meeting	Robert Lyon (sample)	Online	Paid

Figure 6-21. *Showing related records*

Returning JSON or XML

In this section, I discuss how to use the Liquid template as a web service that returns JSON or XML. This is useful in scenarios where you must pass the data to another system, for instance to a payment gateway or to some external system or application to consume the data. These results can be used to develop a complex user experience such as an HTML5 single-page application and Ajax apps. This is achieved through the web template's MIME type property.

Let's create the web template with the same FetchXML code that was used in the previous example.

```
<fetch version="1.0" output-format="xml-platform"
mapping="logical" distinct="false">
  <entity name="sbma_eventregistration">
    <attribute name="sbma_name" />
    <attribute name="sbma_registrationstatus" />
    <attribute name="sbma_paymentoption" />
    <attribute name="sbma_membercontactid" />
    <attribute name="sbma_eventid" />
    <attribute name="sbma_eventregistrationid" />
    <order attribute="sbma_name" descending="false" />
    <link-entity name="sbma_event" from="sbma_eventid"
    to="sbma_eventid" visible="false" link-type="outer"
    alias="events">
      <attribute name="sbma_name" />
      <attribute name="sbma_eventcode" />
    </link-entity>
  </entity>
</fetch>
{% endfetchxml %}

{"EventRegistrations":
  [
    {% for registrations in eventRegistrations.results.entities %}
    {
      "EventCode": "{{registrations['events.sbma_
      eventcode']}}",
      "RegistrationCode":"{{registrations.sbma_name}}",
      "PaymentOption":"{{registrations.sbma_paymentoption.
      Label}}",
      "RegistrationStatus":"{{registrations.sbma_
      registrationstatus.Label}}"
    }
```

```
{% unless forloop.last %}, {% endunless %}
{% endfor %}
]
}
```

The unless tag of Liquid is used to add the comma between each result it returns. If this is not done, you will get a JSON formatting error. You can see the JSON formatting highlighted here. The most important thing is to set the MIME type, as shown in Figure 6-22.

Figure 6-22. *Setting the MIME type*

You must create the page template and the web page without the header and footer to access the service. As per this example, the following URL can be used to access the service: `https://sbmamembership. microsoftcrmportals.com/EventRegSvc/`.

If you go to the Developer Tools of the browser, you can see the results, as shown in Figure 6-23.

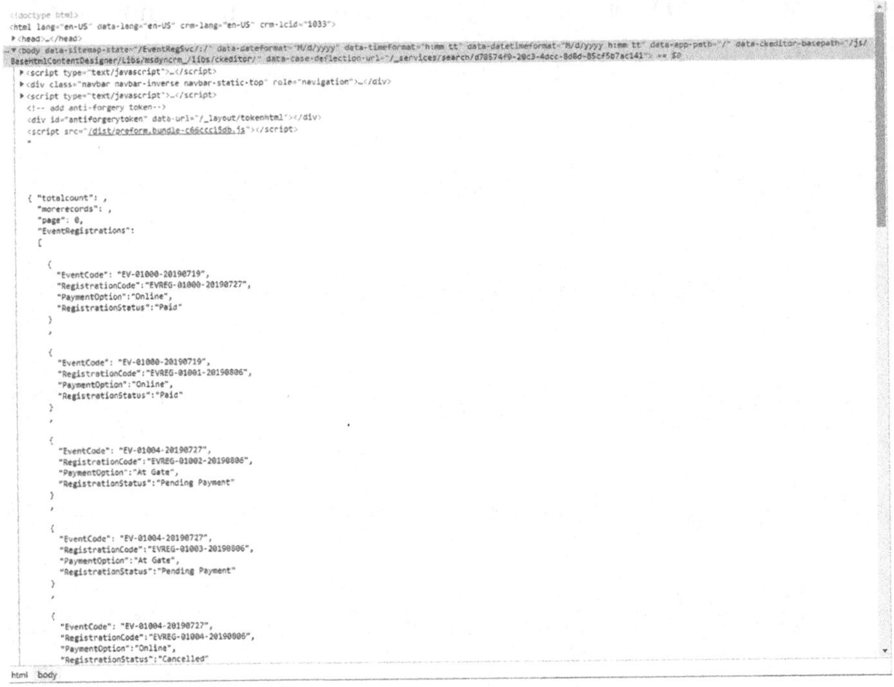

Figure 6-23. *Browser's Developer Tools view of the result*

To retrieve data as XML, you need to change the code as follows. Basically, create the XML tags for the result set and change the MIME type to application/XML.

```
{% fetchxml eventRegistrations %}
<fetch version="1.0" output-format="xml-platform"
mapping="logical" distinct="false">
```

```
    <entity name="sbma_eventregistration">
      <attribute name="sbma_name" />
      <attribute name="sbma_registrationstatus" />
      <attribute name="sbma_paymentoption" />
      <attribute name="sbma_membercontactid" />
      <attribute name="sbma_eventid" />
      <attribute name="sbma_eventregistrationid" />
      <order attribute="sbma_name" descending="false" />
      <link-entity name="sbma_event" from="sbma_eventid"
      to="sbma_eventid" visible="false" link-type="outer"
      alias="events">
        <attribute name="sbma_name" />
        <attribute name="sbma_eventcode" />
      </link-entity>
    </entity>
</fetch>
{% endfetchxml %}
<?xml version="1.0" encoding="UTF-8" ?>
<fetchxmlquery>
  <totalcount>{{ eventRegistrations.results.total_record_count }}
  </totalcount>
  <morerecords>{{ eventRegistrations.results.more_records }}
  </morerecords>
  <page>{{ request.params['page'] | default: 0 }}</page>
  <results>
    {% for registrations in eventRegistrations.results.entities %}
      <registrations>
        <EventCode>{{registrations['events.sbma_
        eventcode']}}<EventCode>
        <RegistrationCode>{{registrations.sbma_name}}
        <RegistrationCode>
```

```
<PaymentOption>{{registrations.sbma_paymentoption.
Label}}<PaymentOption>
<RegistrationStatus>{{registrations.sbma_
registrationstatus.Label}}<RegistrationStatus>
  </registrations>
{% endfor %}
  </results>
</fetchxmlquery>
```

The highlighted code is for formatting the XML. You can query the page using the URL that was demonstrated in the previous example. When you open the browser's developer window, then you can see the XML output, as illustrated in Figure 6-24.

Figure 6-24. *XML result set viewed in browser's Developer Tools view*

Important   Sometimes you might have to deal with large queries that exceed the 5,000-record limit of FetchXML. In such scenarios, you should be using the paging cookie to query a larger data set gracefully. The following URL provides the mechanism for how to deal with such scenarios efficiently: `https://community.dynamics.com/365/b/colinvermandermicrosoft/posts/dynamics-365-portal-use-liquid-fetchxml-with-paging-cookie.`

Deploying Portal Files

In this section, you will quickly learn how to deploy portal files. All the configuration that we do will be saved to the CDS (Common Data Services). So, how would you release the work to the target environments? The process is simple, and the good old XRMToolBox has two options.

Portal Configuration Deployer

This plug-in allows you to select the source and the target environment to deploy your configuration (Figure 6-25). You can select the configurations in the source and click the Import button on the toolbar, and the configuration will be imported to the target.

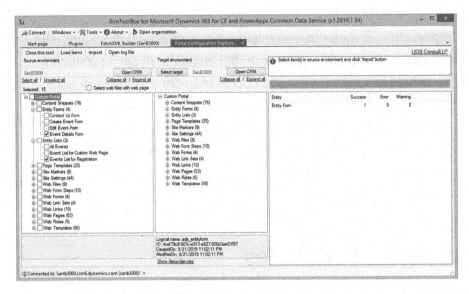

Figure 6-25. *Portal Configuration Deployer tool*

The primary benefit of this tool is that you can pick the configuration that you want to deploy. For instance, sometimes not all configurations needs to be released, only one or two. This is useful in application support scenarios where you can release a minor configuration very quickly.

Portal Records Mover

This plug-in is ideal for moving a configuration as a whole. For instance, if you are tasked with setting up a new test environment for the portal that should be like your existing dev/test environment, you can export all the configurations to one XML file using this plug-in. Once the configuration is exported, it can be imported to any environment.

The "Import records" button on the toolbar (Figure 6-26) will open the import configuration window, as you can see in Figure 6-27.

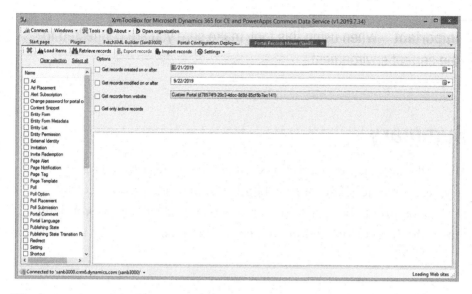

Figure 6-26. *Portal Records Mover tab*

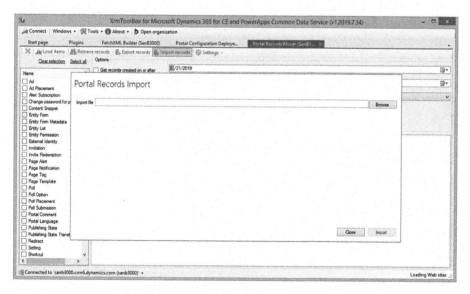

Figure 6-27. *Portal Records Import screen*

Important   When using this tool, make sure you are connected to the correct environment.

Summary

This is the last chapter of this book, and I have demonstrated a few complex examples of how to use Liquid templates. This chapter was focused on how to build more complex web portals that are beyond the out-of-the-box customizations and configurations.

Index

A, B

Account scope, 77
AlexaCRM, 7
Arrays, 181–182
ASMX web service, 166
Azure Active Directory B2C
   portal configuration
      claims mapping, 70
      login screen, 72
      open ID connect
        protocol, 69
      password configuration, 70
      sign-in page, 71, 72
      single identity provider, 70
      site settings, 69, 71
   tenant (*see* Azure Active
      Directory B2C tenant)
   values, 60
Azure Active Directory B2C tenant
   applications, 63
   application setting, 64
   Azure subscription, 62
   creation, 61, 62
   home page, 61
   identity providers, 66
   key generation, 64, 65
   switch directory, 63
   user attributes and claims, 67
   user flow, 65–68

C

Community portal template, 2, 3
Contact-based authentication
   external (*see* External
      authentication)
   user registration, 38
      access control, 41
      access page, 40
      admin login, 41, 42
      contact selection, 40, 44
      login page, 38
      new portal editor, 42, 43
      password changing, 43
      profile page, 39
      web page, 41
Contact scope, 76, 77
Content management systems
   (CMSs), 5
Custom code
   HTML code, 142, 143
   JavaScript editor, 143, 144
   jQuery, 142

© Sanjaya Yapa 2019
S. Yapa, *Getting Started with Dynamics 365 Portals*,
https://doi.org/10.1007/978-1-4842-5346-5

Printed in the United States
By Bookmasters